THE
LOWFAT
LIFESTYLE

- **DELICIOUS LOWFAT RECIPES**
- **HEALTH & FITNESS TIPS**
- **KEEP-TRIM EXERCISES**

by Valerie Parker & Ronda Gates

FOREWORD BY COVERT BAILEY
author of *THE FIT-OR-FAT
TARGET DIET*

Many thanks to our families whose encouragement and patience allowed us to persevere and to our friends who have shared favorite recipes with us.

Special appreciation is expressed to Dr. Herman Frankel for his thoughtful critique and helpful suggestions.

Cover Design: Carol McKasson

Typesetting and Printing: Catalogs Unlimited, Inc.
Hillsboro, Oregon 97123

First printing, February 1984

Revised Edition
Second printing, July 1984
Third printing, September 1984
Fourth printing, January 1985

Library of Congress Number: 84-242769

ISBN 0-9613838-0-1

LFL ASSOCIATES
17131 Hofer Court, Lake Oswego, Oregon 97034

TABLE OF CONTENTS

ABOUT THE AUTHORS

RONDA GATES is the owner of Systems Fitness, a company that provides health enhancement programs to the Oregon corporate and public community. She is a workshop leader for Covert Bailey Seminars and serves as Fitness Consultant to Providence Hospital, Portland, Oregon. Her original degree in Pharmacology has been supplemented with advanced courses in anatomy, kinesiology, psychology, exercise physiology and movement education. She is certified by the American College of Sports Medicine as a Fitness Leader and is a graduate of Covert Bailey's Training Clinic where she was certified to provide exercise and nutrition counselling and conduct body fat testing. Ms. Gates is an appointed member of the Oregon Governor's Council on Health, Fitness and Sports, is active in the International Dance Exercise Association and serves on the national board of the Association for Fitness in Business. She resides in Portland, Oregon, with her husband, Mark, and two children, Rebecca and Caleb. Her interests beyond her work include dance, theater, outdoor sports, beach walking, mountain sitting and reading historical fiction.

VALERIE PARKER has both undergraduate and graduate degrees in Physiology. Several years of cancer research at Stanford were followed by further study at UCLA. She has been a member of the medical support staff at Health Maintenance Organization, specializing in blood disorders. Encouraged by a husband who appreciates good food, her interest in and flair for cooking has been developed through experimentation, formal entertainment and participation in gourmet groups. She lives with her husband, Ron, in Lake Oswego, Oregon, where she enjoys growing and cooking her own tomatoes, and picking and preserving Oregon fruits. Other interests include aerobic dancing, cross-country skiing, hiking, camping, picnicking and reading mystery novels.

FOREWORD

The major health problems in our society today are not hypertension or heart disease or diabetes or even cancer. Although these syndromes are listed as the major causes of death in the United States, it is an underlying cause of these diseases — obesity — that we should be treating, not its effects after disease strikes. Most of the diseases that are associated with obesity could be prevented with a combination of diet and exercise.

Fitness is not a fad. Americans are practical. They know a good thing when they experience it. Anyone who embarks on a regular program of aerobic exercise and prudent diet can expect significant physical and emotional benefits. The key is in realizing that the two go together. Diet helps to rid us of pounds of excess body fat. Exercise changes our insides by making our metabolism more efficient.

There are lots of recipe and fitness books around but here is one that keeps things in perspective. For one thing, cooking tasty food is a shallow activity if the foods lead to obesity. These recipes attack the prime fattening ingredient of our diet — FAT. Anything you cook using this book will be fun and nutritious without being full of fat and sugar. Best of all, there are exercise hints sprinkled here and there so that you won't forget about that other aspect of good health. What a pleasure to see a recipe book that doesn't concentrate so hard on foods that the reader forgets the restorative effects of exercise.

Use this book for great eating and good exercise and join those of us who are getting the most out of life.

Good luck,

Covert Bailey

Lake Tahoe, CA, 1984

vii

PREFACE

Can people lose fat and keep it off?

Today, the answer is "YES".

Until very recently, people who wanted to lose body fat and keep it off had very little reason for optimism. In even the most successful weight loss programs, not more than six out of every hundred people who lost twenty pounds were able to maintain that weight loss for a whole year; only three were able to keep it off for two years.

These discouraging results were not due to lack of motivation, or will-power, or moral fiber, or intelligence. Only in recent years, as we have begun to put together the results of research done in different fields, have we begun to understand why some of the most widely-used approaches to weight loss were rarely helpful. High-intensity exercise doesn't teach our bodies how to burn our body fat for fuel; instead, it usually makes us very hungry. Starving ourselves doesn't teach our bodies how to use up our body fat; instead, it usually forces us to burn our own muscle tissue as well as fat, usually leaves us weak and miserable, and, after we "go off our diets", usually results in our being worse off than before because we've put on fat to replace the fat and muscle that we lost. Relying on weight-loss "diets", or special "diet foods", doesn't help us develop lifetime habits of enjoyable, wholesome eating that will delight us and our families and our friends; instead, it usually leaves us feeling deprived, isolated, and resentful. Cultivating feelings of guilt and shame in an effort to stop ourselves from doing what we "should not" be doing doesn't lead to changes that are safe, effective, enjoyable and lasting; usually, it sets the stage for our abandoning the effort yet again, and feeling even worse about ourselves than before.

Valerie Parker and Ronda Gates here offer a cheerful, upbeat treasury of practical ideas about eating, shopping, cooking, and exercising, practical ideas that can help anyone begin to move beyond the limitations of the fat in our food and the limitations of the fat in our bodies. They share the recipes and techniques that they have developed, tested and found useful in reducing fat intake down to 30% of the day's calories, in accordance with the Dietary Goals for the United States and the advice of the American Heart Association. Their book shows how to start enjoying food again: food that is a pleasure to prepare, to serve, and to eat. Their recipes and suggestions are useful tools that can help anyone develop new skills and renewed confidence.

A note of caution: be gentle with yourself; let yourself take the steps you feel comfortable taking, and give yourself permission to choose personal goals that are big enough to matter and small enough to achieve safely and gracefully. Let yourself take the steps you're ready to take, and give yourself permission to make progress at a pace that feels exactly right to you.

Enjoy.

Herman M. Frankel, M.D.

Portland, Oregon 1984

(Dr. Frankel is co-director of the Kaiser Permanente Health Services Research Center's *Freedom From Fat* program. This highly successful two-year campaign gained national attention in 1984 after receiving the US Secretary of Health and Human Services Award for Excellence in Community Health Promotion and Disease Prevention.)

INTRODUCTION

THE LOWFAT LIFESTYLE is a collaborative effort by two people who like to eat and who have discovered, after years of struggling with the battle of the bulge, tools and techniques to enable them to attain and maintain optimum levels of body fat and desirable weight goals!

Like most Americans, Ronda Gates and Valerie Parker knew that regular exercise and a prudent diet were the keys to looking and feeling good. Ronda taught ten hours of aerobic dance classes weekly and invested considerable amounts of time studying extensively in the field of health and fitness. Eager to share her new-found knowledge, she spent non-teaching hours putting the information she had acquired into lay terms in the form of newsletters for her students. Meanwhile, she thought she ate well and because she exercised so much she indulged her sweet tooth daily.

Valerie was a student at the first aerobic dance class that Ronda offered. As an experienced cook she felt she used good judgment in her daily food choices...3 square meals a day, fewer sauces, less emphasis on sweets and more on fresh fruits and vegetables. She struggled with some extra pounds now and then in the classic "yo-yo" syndrome (pounds up, pounds down, pounds up) but like Ronda had a respectable size 11 frame.

Although they weren't preoccupied with their appearance both yearned for a more compact package. In May, 1983, the results of hydrostatic weighing to determine body fat content showed that they carried sufficient muscle for their frames but were above optimum levels of body fat, which was probably why they were dissatisfied with their physical appearance. Independently, they both realized it was time to re-evaluate their diet and exercise regimen because something was definitely wrong.

The following week Ronda attended a five-day Training Clinic offered by Covert Bailey, a nutritional biochemist from M.I.T. who had authored a best-selling book, FIT OR FAT? and who introduced his newest publication, THE FIT-OR-FAT TARGET DIET. The discussion of body fat evaluation, exercise, diet and nutrition, combined with her years of study, showed Ronda how to improve her eating habits to attain optimum health and led her to introduce workshops on similar subjects for her own students.

Valerie was a participant at the first Target Diet workshop and quickly became convinced of the merits of making one significant change in her eating habits — decreasing dietary fat intake. Drawing on her cooking expertise, she set out to develop delicious new recipes and adapt old favorites to reflect a lower fat content. As their eating habits changed, both found themselves slimming down. A repeat of the hydrostatic weighing experience showed that their efforts had paid off. Both had dropped body fat levels without losing any muscle!

Valerie and Ronda had discovered that it is possible to become and stay slim without dieting. They have shared their experiences and knowledge to produce THE LOWFAT LIFESTYLE, a book combining health and fitness information with tasty, de-fatted recipes.

This is not a "diet" by the common definition which implies a regimen of eating specific foods for a limited time in order to drop pounds quickly. It doesn't promise magic results in two weeks and it doesn't call for radical changes in what you eat. Instead, the book will give you an understanding of how the body utilizes its daily nutrients and the importance of the right kind of exercise in this process. Small changes in the way you cook and go about your daily routine WILL result in a healthier, lowfat life.

There is added benefit to this way of living. For years authorities such as the American Heart Association, medical researchers and registered dietitians have been advising Americans, especially those with a perceived risk of having a heart attack, to lower their blood cholesterol levels. Reducing the amount of fat in the diet, especially saturated fat, reduces the amount of cholesterol. In general, the fattier the food, the greater its cholesterol content is likely to be.

The American Heart Association, in 1984, looked at new evidence and now strongly recommends that ALL Americans should significantly reduce the amount of fat in their diet, to a maximum of 30%. U.S. Dietary Goals also recommend a diet that consists of 20-30% fat. Following THE LOWFAT LIFESTYLE will help you easily attain this level, lose inches and still enjoy your favorite foods.

Following a lowfat lifestyle means lowering your dietary intake of fat and physiologically increasing the fat burning capability of your body through a regular aerobic exercise program. The key word is "lifestyle", implying a permanent change in the way you live rather than the temporary quick-fix of a crash diet or exercise course.

Approximate calories and fat grams have been calculated for the recipes, and nutrition and cooking tips are scattered throughout the book. In addition to lowfat recipes you will find many with an emphasis on increased fiber and decreased sugar consumption, as recommended by current authorities. Ideas for behavioral changes to increase your physical activity level and specific, keep-trim exercises have been included to remind you that a change in the way you eat is only part of the answer.

We hope this book will provide you with the insight to make your own exciting changes, create delicious new recipes and ultimately enjoy a new, lowfat lifestyle!

FOOD FADS AND FACTS

DON'T BE A DIET YO-YO!

How many of you can say you've lost a couple of hundred pounds?

Your initial reaction may be thank goodness you've never been so out of control that you acquired that much excess baggage. On the other hand, many of us have lost a couple of hundred pounds in our lives. Not all at once, but by living a "yo-yo" existence. Down five and up six, down five and up five, down ten and up ten. It all adds up to a couple of hundred pounds over 20 years. Fortunately, that syndrome can disappear once you learn more about calorie sources and the way to choose and cook foods that make it easier to control your weight. The pounds will remain lost and your body shape will stabilize.

Most people have very little understanding of how the body reacts to the extremes of eating and dieting. They don't realize that body metabolism changes when exposed to the quick weight loss schemes that most of us have experienced.

You're 42 years old. You've known it was coming and it finally arrives — the invitation to your 25th high school reunion. Be honest — isn't your immediate reaction, "I wonder what everyone looks like"? That's followed by a look at yourself and possibly, "What do I look like?" If you've been eating carefully and exercising regularly chances are you're in good shape. The reality of the situation is more likely that your exercise routine may not be the kind that utilizes body fat stores or your eating habits aren't all that great and your diet is still too high in fat.

Measurement of the body fat of an increasing number of aerobic exercisers indicates that most active people have adequate amounts of lean muscle mass, an indication that they exercise regularly at an exertion level that should utilize their body fat stores. However, these same measurements show that their body fat remains about 5-7% above optimum levels. This gives them a little bit more in the inch department than they like — accompanied by what they believe to be a 10 pound weight surplus. More important, it's a clear indication that their regular exercise program hasn't been accompanied with proper food choices — low in fat, low in sugar, high in fiber — supplied as a balanced diet.

But, back to the reunion. You are determined that when you return to your friends of long ago, you're going to look fabulous. Never mind that it's vanity on parade...it's also human nature on parade. We all want to convince everyone we've moved forward in our lives since we left high school.

You choose to embark on the long delayed TOTAL regimen of proper exercise and diet. You may even have some idea of how to do it. But time slips away and what began as a six month program becomes a three month program and then lo and behold, where did the time go...the reunion is a month away and you've still not pulled yourself together.

So, what do you do? Return to a good old reliable quick weight loss plan. Throw all the good sense out the window — it doesn't matter if you lose lean muscle or fat — you're just determined to get into that size 10 dress or the pants with the 34 inch waist and good health be damned.

You go on the Beverly Hills Diet, or the Cambridge Diet or the Stillman Diet or the Banana Diet. It doesn't matter. The good news is IT WORKS! Four weeks later you attend the reunion in the outfit you thought you'd never get into. As a matter of fact, you knock them on their ears and have a marvelous time to boot. But here's the bad news. Let's find out what you've done to yourself to get there and how you're going to pay.

When a person who maintains a 2200 calorie intake on a regular basis embarks on a quick weight loss scheme that restricts caloric intake to less than 1200 calories for a woman or 1500 calories for a man, the body reacts with shock. Your inside voice says, "My goodness, what's happening here? A famine must have struck — I've not seen a decent morsel of food for 24 hours." Then the next day comes and with your will power holding steady the body cries out in alarm, "This is serious business, all systems on alert — emergency procedures get ready — the food situation isn't looking at all good!"

At this point the body metabolism responds by shutting down. It slows to a level that allows you to maintain all your normal body functions. For our purposes let's assume it drops to an 800 calorie burning level. Remember how tired you were on the first few days of a restrictive diet? The body has slowed so much that you have less energy for your daily routine.

Slowed metabolism be damned, you've lost weight. You lost ten pounds of weight very quickly. In reality, you lost about five pounds of water (you knew that — you've spent your life in the bathroom!), three pounds of fat and two pounds of valuable muscle protein. (Valuable because muscle is what burns calories, and when you have less of it your capacity to burn calories is diminished.)

Reunion day arrives and you don't have to starve any more. In fact, you have a few too many beers and pile in the hors d'oeuvres and pretend that you eat like this all year round! Meantime your body is saying, "Reprieve! We are not in a prison camp. She must have confessed because they are letting her eat!"

But it's also saying, "Beware! This food business could end at any time — we'd better stay on alert and keep our metabolic rate low and store these excess calories as fat for the coming and continuing famine!" Your body, which has been pumping along at an 800 calorie burning level continues to do so as you gorge yourself with food then return to your normal level of 2200 calories a day. However, those 2200 calories are no longer maintenance calories. They are 1400 EXCESS calories and we all know that excess calories are stored as fat.

The worst news is that the body does not respond as quickly to the increase in calories as it did to the decrease in calories. It continues to see your normal calorie intake as excessive for several weeks and that's why you gain all your weight back so quickly — and often add a few pounds for good measure.

Not only that, but the ten pounds come back on as five pounds of water and five pounds of grease! You end up fatter than you were to start with even if you don't weigh more. And, since fat weight is more bulky than muscle weight you are physically bigger even though you weigh the same as you did before you started to diet. You repeat the syndrome over and over again. In time, it adds up to a bulkier you!

You think this can't be true? A methodical system of providing the body with four days of excess calories in combination with four days of extreme caloric restriction is one of the most effective ways of treating people who have difficulty GAINING weight! It works for them and it will work for you!

The human body is the most complex and efficient "machine" known to man. It is designed for survival. As long as we treat it well, keep it cleaned, mechanically tuned (with proper exercise), carefully fed (with good food choices), and support its psychological and social needs, chances are we can assure ourselves of looking and feeling good most every day of our lives. Even if you lead a hectic life, in business or as a homemaker, good eating habits combined with a regular exercise program can pay off. No more yo-yo! Remember, it's only this practical combination that will enable you to attain the mental and physical image to which you aspire!

LOSING THE POINT

Anyone who lectures on the nutritional aspects of a lowfat lifestyle continually gets questions that deal with what I call the quackery fringe that sits on the side of a very straightforward and simple concept.

"Isn't honey better than sugar because it is more 'natural' and has more nutrients?"

"Doesn't iron bind with certain foods that make it unable to be released for absorption by the body?"

"Aren't we better off eating margarine instead of butter?"

"If it's so important to have milk in the diet how do so many nations survive on a milk-free diet?"

"If eggs are so bad for you how come much of the WW II population survived on a diet consisting primarily of eggs without developing cardiac disease?"

"Isn't raw milk better for us than pasteurized?"

The questions go on and on and it's my guess everyone has had a similar notion on some issue at some time. I'm embarrassed to admit I once believed it was important to eat as many eggs for breakfast as pieces of bacon...it was part of some kind of weight loss plan that combined foods...I don't even remember where that rumor came from.

That's the problem. We draw one little item from a total concept and focus on it, losing sight of the forest because of one tree.

The rules for a balanced diet have been time-tested and are quite simple. Daily goals for most of us are two servings of foods that supply the nutrients found in meat products, two servings of the foods known as dairy products, four servings of grain products and four of fruits and vegetables. The U.S. Senate Select Committee on Nutrition and Human Needs has published reasonable and prudent Dietary Goals that encourage us to eat a variety of foods, maintain ideal weight, avoid too much fat and cholesterol, eat more complex carbohydrates, avoid too much sugar and sodium and, if we drink alcohol, to do so in moderation.

Nutritional biochemist Covert Bailey has taken these goals one step further by developing a nutrition education program that describes a way to choose food that conforms to these criteria by focusing on a balanced selection of foods low in fat, low in sugar and high in fiber. Regardless of the tool we use, our personal goal should be to get ALL the nutrients we need EVERY day by eating a reasonable and prudent diet comprised of a variety of wonderful, satisfying, healthy and delicious foods!

R.G.

WHY AREN'T THEY HEALTHY?

A recent article in Medical Tribune (May 12, 1982) took a look at adolescents aged 12 to 16 who had low levels of iron, riboflavin and vitamin C. It seems these young people had significantly less aerobic capacity than same-age children who weren't deficient.

When the first group was given daily supplements of vitamin C, riboflavin and iron, they improved noticeably, causing one scientist to say those three nutrients "may be associated with tissue processes affecting physical fitness".

These findings may well be true. However, in the belief that we should be treating the underlying disease rather than the symptoms, it is important to look at WHY teenagers acquire nutritional deficiencies instead of just deciding to give them vitamin and mineral supplements.

Teenagers rarely eat a well-balanced diet. It is possible that their haphazard eating patterns predispose them to a variety of minor illnesses, mood changes and nutritional deficiencies.

How can you, as a parent, help them? If you struggle with your teenagers' diet, you may provide them with another factor against which to rebel. But if you are aware that they are "junk-fooding" their way through the day when they are away from home, at least try to make lowfat, low sugar, high fiber foods available when they are at home.

Sober, responsible, valid and legitimate research findings are appropriate only in the setting in which they are made. They are not always applicable to the general setting in which most of us live every day. Suppose as a result of this study we found ourselves re-evaluating how we deal with the daily eating habits of our teenagers. Wouldn't the bottom line be that instead of giving them a vitamin and mineral supplement every day we might decide that it would be lot better to educate them to the benefits of eating a balanced diet that would assure their aerobic capacity — and their good health?

Scientific conclusions do seem impractical sometimes!

A WORD ABOUT VITAMINS

Americans place too much dependence on commercial vitamin sources. We look to vitamin and mineral supplements or chemical substances to prevent or fix any number of ailments — real or imagined.

Vitamin sales are a million dollar business yet there is no such thing as the perfect or complete vitamin on the market today. If there were one perfect substitute for the nutrients provided us in food, you can be sure that everyone would know about it.

A recent search through health food stores, natural food stores, chain drug stores and vitamin specialty stores did not turn up any multivitamin that fulfilled the minimum daily requirements for more than seven of the fifty nutrients we need every day.

Vitamins do play an important role in treating some disease processes, as a supplement for people under the physical and mental stress of some illnesses and in assuring adequate amounts of certain nutrients in some populations. However, if you are in reasonable health, your best source for attaining all the vitamins you need is a balanced diet, particularly one with an abundance of fresh food, which provides more nutrients than any other food form.

This is not to say that a multivitamin supplement is impractical or even unreasonable. But we simply cannot provide our bodies with the nutrients we need EVERY day by taking a pill. Besides, food is so wonderful!

Instead of supporting the pharmaceutical industry in this area, let's eat more fresh fruits and vegetables, more whole grains and a balanced diet. The satisfaction of living every day of your life the best you can — emotionally, physically and nutritionally — will allow you to reap the benefits of a lowfat lifestyle.

GETTING STARTED

WHAT ARE FATS?

Fats are our most concentrated energy source. A gram of fat provides nine (9) calories. In addition to providing energy (their most important role), fats allow the fat soluble vitamins (A, D, E and K) to ride piggy-back to their point of utilization. Fat is essential to prevent a deficiency of linoleic acid, an essential nutrient which is needed for normal growth and nerve function and synthesis of hormone-like substances called prostaglandins.

Most dietary fats are present as triglycerides, some as phospholipids and sterols. Fatty foods get their flavor from the fatty acids that comprise the triglycerides. Fatty acids may be saturated (primarily from animal sources and usually in solid form) or unsaturated (primarily from plant sources and usually in liquid form). (See chart at the end of this section.)

As a result of education on heart disease, most people believe that they are better off eating polyunsaturated fats than saturated fats and there is some real evidence that this is true. However, switching to oils that are polyunsaturated and not cutting down on the quantity of fats is not the answer. FATS ARE FATS and Americans consume far too many, contributing not only to heart disease but to obesity and a wide range of other medical problems.

Remember, fats are an essential part of our diet, but in reasonable quantities, please!

Americans often eat over 45% of their diet as fat calories. U.S. DIETARY GOALS RECOMMEND A DIET THAT IS 20 — 30% FAT. This is a suitable level for people who are already optimally lean. Overfat people may need to eat less fat until they get fit.

15

OVERWEIGHT OR OVERFAT?

GREASY! SLIMY! OILY! WAXY!
MESSY! FATTY! DIRTY! SMEARY!

Great words, huh? Let's talk about weighing that stuff and finding out what you're really made of!

Did you know that bathroom scales are becoming obsolete? That's because your weight doesn't necessarily say much about how fat you are or the state of your general physical condition. For example, you could be a 98 pound weakling and still be obese.

The critical issue is your percentage of body fat. This is the ratio of the fat in your body to everything else you carry — muscles, bones, hair, teeth, air, water, etc. Ideally, the percentage of body fat compared to lean body mass should be around 15% for a man and 22% for a woman. The average American male is over 25% fat, and female over 30% fat. Obviously most of us are carrying around far more fat than we need!!

The problem is that even trim looking people can have a lot of fat both under their skin (known as subcutaneous fat) or embedded in their muscles (as Covert Bailey describes it, "like marbling in a steak") and get fooled by the scales into thinking they are not fat. You can be confused by the message your scale gives you when you begin to exercise or lift weights. As the intramuscular fat is burned off and is replaced with more dense muscle tissue, the scale may show "no weight loss today" or may show a weight gain, even though you are less fat and probably more healthy.

There are many ways to measure obesity, including scales, which measure weight, and those tools which measure fat. There are many people who think they are overweight who are not. They have lots of lean body mass, particularly muscle, that makes their body frames large. There are also many people who think they are normal weight (or even skinny) but who actually carry over 30% fat in and on their body (way too much). And there are some who are both overweight and overfat.

Medical personnel for years have been concerned about the plight of patients who are overweight. Happily, they are now realizing that scales aren't the only things that count. It's important to know how much fat their patients carry around as well.

The only way to know for sure how much body fat you have is to have it measured. There are a number of ways to have this done, some more or less sophisticated. The two most popular are hydrostatic weighing and skin fold calibration.

Hydrosystatic or underwater weighing makes use of the principle that fat floats, and is considered a very accurate tool for measuring body fat! Because muscles, bones and other tissues are more dense than body fat, the more of this lean body tissue you carry, the more you will weigh when submerged in water. We all know how oil sits on top of water — the same principle applies to measuring body fat — too much fat and you float! Hydrostatic weighing can be a very motivating experience for setting lower body fat or higher lean muscle goals. Fortunately, there are an increasing number of facilities that offer this service, so look for them in your area.

A more common test is done with skin-fold calipers. This tool gently pinches the skin at different sites on the body. The results are computed to determine your approximate percentage of body fat. A skilled "pincher" or one who uses an electronic caliper can give fairly accurate results. Regardless of the tool used, the goal is to measure the change over a period of time.

Knowing your percentage of body fat can enable you to set reasonable goals for diet and exercise. These are the only factors that can alter your percentage of body fat. People who carry sufficient lean body tissue but too much fat can continue to exercise at an exertion level that George Sheehan describes as "the perceived level of exertion." This is a pace that raises the pulse above resting levels but is not so fast that you are out of breath or cannot talk to a companion. These people also need to lower the fat content of their diet. On the other hand, a person who carries too much fat AND too little muscle will have to embark on an aerobic exercise program using perceived levels of exertion, alter the fat content of the diet and lift weights to increase the muscle mass of the body.

Find out whether you're fat by having your body measured for lean tissue and body fat. It's your best tool for determining if your current exercise and diet regimen is working to keep you lean!

REMEMBER, WHEN IT COMES TO FAT, NOT EVEN YOUR BATHROOM SCALE KNOWS FOR SURE!

MAXIMUM BODY FAT LEVELS
FOR OPTIMUM HEALTH

MALES	15%
FEMALES	22%

GETTING RID OF FAT

An obvious way to get rid of fat is to eat less of it. Common sense tells us that when you eat less fat you are more likely to burn body fat stores and probably decrease your body fat levels more quickly. Well, we've learned that exercise plays the most important role in utilizing body fat depots for energy and cutting the amount of fat we carry on our body. Still the question arises...wouldn't it be even better to eliminate fat from the diet entirely?

The answer is no, and it couldn't be done anyway. The body requires about a 5% fat content in the diet. It's hard to imagine a balanced diet that would be less than 5% fat so the chances of becoming fat deficient are extremely low.

So, we can't have a completely fat-free diet. But perhaps we could lower the fat content of the diet to 10%, for example, in order to make increased use of body fat stores. Lowering the fat content of the diet to this level might be a health-saving measure, but it would also make for a somewhat restricted diet. Since most Americans consume a 40 — 50% fat diet, it's no wonder so many of us are over the optimum body fat goals of 15% for men, 22% for women. In addition, most of us don't get enough aerobic exercise to metabolize the fat already sitting there...we just keep adding it on.

Cutting down to the recommended dietary goal of 20 — 30% fat is much more reasonable, especially if you combine it with a regular aerobic exercise program at least three times a week. Your fat didn't accumulate in one day, week or month and it won't disappear overnight but patience, persistence and perseverance will assure success. Once it's gone you'll realize it was worth the effort!

NUMBERS TO REMEMBER

A 2000 calorie diet which is 20% FAT has 400 fat calories or 44 GRAMS OF FAT (or 9 Covert Bailey Fat Units).

A 2000 calorie diet which is 30% FAT has 600 fat calories or 66 GRAMS OF FAT (or 13 Covert Bailey Fat Units).

SAMPLE CALCULATION FOR A 20% FAT DIET:

2000 calories x 20% = 400 calories

There are 9 calories per gram of fat, so

400 calories divided by 9 = 44 grams of fat

1 Covert Bailey Fat Unit = 5 grams of fat, so

44 grams divided by 5 = 9 Fat Units

SO YOU CAN'T LIVE WITHOUT BUTTER
(OR CREAM, OR MAYO)

No one is asking you to go "cold turkey" on the foods you have come to know and love so well. That's not realistic. There are, however, a number of ways you can make small behavioral changes and help your body discover new ways of enjoying the taste of your favorite foods without the addition of excess fats.

Try cutting the quantities of these "far-out-fat" foods in half. Use teaspoons, not tablespoons. For example, you will note in our recipes that usually only 1 teaspoon of oil, if any, is used to brown a pound of meat. Check your old favorite recipes — most of them probably suggest 2 to 4 tablespoons of oil per pound! That's not necessary!

One of your goals is to re-educate your palate. Learn how to replace one habit with another. If you LOVE mayonnaise, butter, cream cheese, avocado, confronting the task of lowfat eating may seem almost insurmountable because you enjoy these foods so much. With small changes over a period of time, you can succeed.

Habitual choices of cheese high in fat can be changed. Try skim milk cheese in place of your regular ones. If cheddar is a special weakness, buy the strongest, sharpest brand available and you'll find you will be satisfied with a smaller amount. Half the amount called for will produce good results in most recipes.

Instead of thickly spreading margarine or mayonnaise on a sandwich, use a lighter hand and a lighter spread. Try our Mock Sour Cream or Mustard-Mayo Cream. If you must have mayonnaise, use one of the reduced-fat brands or add nonfat yogurt to the jar in increasing quantities as you use it up — you may find that you can fill the mayo jar with yogurt and hardly notice the difference. Use the same trick for sour cream: yogurt (with a bit of lemon juice) makes a very acceptable substitute. Do you think that buttermilk is mostly fat? (After all, look at that name.) It's not — most brands are fat-free. And salad dressings made with buttermilk and nonfat yogurt or lowfat cottage cheese are both low in fat and delicious!

It's hard to find a substitute for an avocado! If that happens to be one of your weaknesses the best bet is to gradually cut quantities. You don't have to give it up in one week or one month or completely. It may take six months of slowly cutting down before you find that one slice will satisfy you — especially combined with other lowfat foods to make it last longer. Actually, just reminding yourself that it is 90% fat will help!

When you examine your own high fat habits, think about how you can re educate your palate.

YOUR GOAL IS A PERMANENT LIFESTYLE CHANGE,
NOT A TEMPORARY QUICK-FIX.

RANKING OF FAT SATURATION

	% Poly-Unsaturated	% Mono-Unsaturated	% Saturated
Safflower Oil	78	12	10
Soybean Oil	63	21	16
Cottonseed Oil	59	16	25
Corn Oil	58	31	11
Peanut Oil	31	46	23
Crisco	26	49	25
Palm Oil	18	32	50
Lard	10	52	38
Olive Oil	7	81	12
Butter	4	37	59
Coconut Oil	0	8	92

CHOICES — ON YOUR OWN

Your lowfat lifestyle will involve many new choices. Remember, we're not suggesting that you give up certain foods. There are no "no-no's" in a lowfat lifestyle. You can learn how to make intelligent substitutions and choices in what you eat. For example, you have probably read that fish is generally lower in fat than red meat and may have decided to eat much more fish. That's great — but you can do even more for yourself if you understand that different fish have different fat contents. The number of grams of fat in 3½ ounces of fish can range from 0.1 to over 15!!

The purpose of this chapter is to give you lists of CHOICES and let you make the final decision. Calorie and fat gram counts have been gathered from a variety of printed sources and some of the numbers may be different from charts you have read or from nutritional information on food labels. Methods of measurement vary from authority to authority but relative values will remain the same. That's what we're interested in at this point, so don't worry about minor discrepancies. Do learn to read labels when choosing between different brands of food in the supermarket. (See the section, LABELS — REQUIRED READING.)

Before you look at the lists of food choices, take the quiz on the next page to test your current understanding of how much fat is contained in various foods. You may be pleasantly surprised at your knowledge — or horrified!

WHERE'S THE FAT?!

Test your knowledge with this simple quiz and make your best guess. Answers are on the next page.

1. Which meal would be lower in fat?
   a. Poached chinook salmon
   b. Roast pork tenderloin

2. Which canned salmon is lower in fat?
   a. Pink salmon
   b. Sockeye salmon

3. Which lunch meat will be lower in fat?
   a. Dry salami
   b. Boiled ham

4. Which would add less fat when spread on your sandwich?
   a. Miracle Whip salad dressing
   b. Whipped margarine

5. To brown mushrooms, which will add less fat?
   a. Regular margarine
   b. Vegetable oil

6. The cravings have got you — which would be lower in fat?
   a. 1 ounce tortilla chips
   b. 1 ounce sunflower seeds

7. You want to improve the taste of your favorite cookies and the recipe suggests adding ¼ cup of one of these. Which would add most fat? Least?
   a. Almonds
   b. Coconut
   c. Raisins

8. You're going to have a Sunday morning egg but have decided to cut out 2 of your usual 4 strips of bacon. Is this now a fairly reasonable lowfat breakfast?
   a. Yes
   b. No

9. How about having 1 frozen waffle or 1 egg — which has less fat?
   a. Waffle
   b. Egg

10 You want a mid-afternoon drink and have a choice of 2% milk or buttermilk — which is the best choice for lowfat sipping?
   a. Milk
   b. Buttermilk

ANSWERS TO QUIZ

1. ROAST PORK TENDERLOIN has less fat, 12.1 grams in 3½ ounces. The same amount of poached chinook salmon has 15.6 grams. Fish is NOT always lower in fat than red meat.

2. PINK SALMON is lower in fat. ⅓ cup of canned pink salmon has 5.9 grams of fat, sockeye has 9.3 grams.

3. BOILED HAM has 4.8 grams of fat per ounce, dry salami has 9.8 grams.

4. MIRACLE WHIP! 7.0 grams per tablespoon, whereas whipped margarine has 8.0 grams. Don't be fooled by words like "whipped"; they don't necessarily imply "lowfat"!

5. REGULAR MARGARINE. It has 11.0 grams of fat per tablespoon, the oil has 14.0 grams.

6. FIGHT down these cravings when possible but if you must have something, choose the TORTILLA CHIPS, at 6 — 8 grams of fat per ounce (depending on brand). The ounce of roasted sunflower seeds will contribute 13.5 grams to your daily total!

7. COCONUT would add the most fat, raisins the least. Per ¼ cup, raisins have 0.1 gram of fat, almonds have 8.5 grams, coconut has 11.8. Be careful when you "throw in a handful" of something.

8. NO. Removing the bacon only cut your fat content by about one third. 2 strips of bacon, fried crisp, contain 8.8 grams, and the egg contributes 6.0 grams! So although the original breakfast would have had 23.6 grams of fat, the "improved" version still has 14.8 grams. Too high for most of us!

9. The WAFFLE is better — 3.0 grams of fat each versus 6.0 grams for the egg. Of course, this assumes you won't pour a tablespoon of butter over your waffle.

10. BUTTERMILK is a better choice. One 8 ounce glass contains almost no fat (0.2 grams) if made from skim milk and only 2.4 grams if made from whole milk. 2% milk, on the other hand, has 4.7 grams of fat in one glass.

Surprised at some of the answers? Take a look at the CHOICES lists that follow to gain a better understanding of relative fat contents of common foods.

CHOICES — MILK PRODUCTS

MILK: (1 cup serving)	FAT GRAMS	CALORIES
Buttermilk, from skim milk	0.2	90
Skim milk	0.4	90
1% milk	2.7	100
2% milk	5.0	120
Whole milk (3.5%)	9.0	160

CREAM: (1 tablespoon)		
Half and half	2.0	20
Sour cream	2.0	25
Heavy or whipping cream	5.6	55

YOGURT: (½ cup)		
Nonfat yogurt	0.4	125
Lowfat yogurt	4.0	140
Regular yogurt	8.0	150

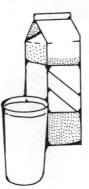

CHOICES — CHEESE

HARD AND SEMI-SOFT: (1 ounce serving)	FAT GRAMS	CALORIES
Cottage Cream Cheese (2 T)*	3.0	50
Mozzarella, part skim	4.5	72
Feta	5.3	84
Parmesan, ¼ cup grated	6.0	100
Neuchatel cream cheese	7.0	70
Gouda	8.0	100
Brie	8.0	94
Swiss	8.0	100
Colby	9.0	110
Roquefort	9.0	105
Cheddar	9.1	112
Cream cheese (2 T)	10.0	100

SOFT: (½ cup serving)		
Cottage cheese, 1%	1.2	80
Cottage cheese, 2% (lowfat)	2.2	100
Cottage cheese, creamed	4.2	106
Ricotta cheese, part skim	9.8	170

* See the LFL recipe for Whipped Cottage Cream Cheese, p. 171.

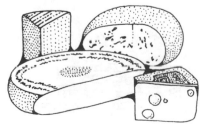

CHOICES — LUNCH MEATS

1 OUNCE SERVING:	FAT GRAMS	CALORIES
Turkey ham	1.5	35
Boiled ham	5.0	66
Salami, cooked	6.0	73
Frankfurter, chicken*	6.5	80
Frankfurter*	7.0	80
Bologna	8.0	88
Liverwurst	9.0	139
Salami, dry	10.0	112

* Note that these numbers are calculated for ONE OUNCE of meat, for comparison purposes. However, frankfurters rarely come as small as one ounce, so one average frankfurter will probably contain more fat than an ounce of any of the other choices listed here.

Be aware that not all products advertised as low in fat really are lowfat. You can see that there is not too much difference between a chicken frank and a regular one on this list. We found one brand of chicken franks, advertised prominently as lowfat, which stated on the label that each frankfurter had 13 grams of fat. This is as high as many brands of regular franks! As the emphasis on lowfat eating spreads, manufacturers will continue to come up with new products in an attempt to capture this growing market. TRY TO GET IN THE HABIT OF READING THE LABEL.

CHOICES — SANDWICH SPREADS

1 TABLESPOON:	FAT GRAMS	CALORIES
Mock Sour Cream*	0.3	15
Catsup	0.3	48
Mustard	0.6	12
Cottage Cream Cheese*	1.5	25
Miracle Whip, lowfat	4.0	45
Mayonnaise, lowfat imitation	5.0	50
Margarine, diet imitation	6.0	50
Miracle Whip salad dressing	7.0	70
Sandwich spread w. pickle	7.2	76
Peanut butter	8.0	95
Margarine, whipped	8.0	70
Margarine, regular	11.0	100
Mayonnaise	11.0	100
Butter	12.0	100
Oil, any kind	14.0	124

* See LFL recipes for Mock Sour Cream, p. 170 , and Whipped Cottage Cream Cheese, p. 171 .

CHOICES — FISH

FRESH FISH: (3½ ounce serving)	FAT GRAMS	CALORIES
Haddock	0.1	79
Cod	0.3	78
Sole	0.5	68
Flounder	0.5	68
Lingcod	0.8	84
Snapper	0.9	93
Halibut	1.2	100
Perch	1.5	95
Sturgeon	1.9	94
Brook trout	2.1	101
Yellowfin tuna	3.0	133
Pink salmon	3.7	119
Swordfish	4.0	118
Pacific mackerel	7.3	159
Butterfish	10.2	169
Atlantic mackerel	12.2	191
Chinook salmon	15.6	222

CANNED FISH: (3 ounce serving)		
Water-packed tuna	0.8	130
Pink salmon	5.9	140
Silver salmon	8.2	150
Oil-packed tuna, drained	8.2	200
Sockeye salmon	9.3	170

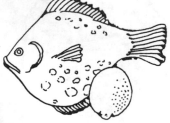

CHOICES — CHICKEN, MEAT, LEGUMES, EGGS

3 OUNCES COOKED: (and trimmed of visible fat)	FAT GRAMS	CALORIES
Chicken, no skin	3.0	115
Beef, top round	4.2	170
Chicken, with skin	5.0	130
Lamb, lean leg	6.0	155
Steak, lean sirloin	6.0	175
Steak, flank	7.0	210
Beef, bottom round	8.2	205
Beef, lean ground	10.0	200
Turkey, ground	11.0	195
Pork, lean roast	12.0	230
Beef, regular ground	17.0	245

LEGUMES:
(1 cup cooked)

	FAT GRAMS	CALORIES
Lentils	0.1	210
Peas, split	0.6	230
Beans, kidney	0.9	220
navy (small white)	1.1	225
pink	1.2	350

EGGS:

	FAT GRAMS	CALORIES
White only	tr	20
Yolk only	5.2	60
Whole	6.0	80

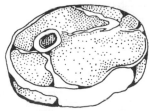

HIGH-FAT SNACKS

When you just can't go a minute longer without a "treat" from your high-fat past, check the list below. Be sure you know exactly what you're doing and how much you're eating!

NUTS AND SEEDS: (1 ounce)	FAT GRAMS	CALORIES
Cashews, about 14 large	13.1	160
Sunflower seeds, 3 Tbsp.	13.5	160
Peanuts, about 30	14.0	170
Walnuts, about 15 halves	15.0	160
Pistachios, about 50	16.0	180
Almonds, about 25	16.2	180
Filberts, about 25	19.0	190
Pecans, about 24 halves	22.0	210
Macadamia nuts, about 12	23.4	220

CHIPS: (1 ounce, about 10)		
Tortilla chips	6-8	160
Potato chips	10-13	150

CHOCOLATE BAR, 1 ounce	10.0	150

FROZEN TREATS: (½ cup serving)		
Sherbet	1.2	130
Ice Milk	3.5	100
Ice Cream, regular	7-10	130
Ice Cream, rich	12-17	165

Many of the popular magazines now include nutritional information with their recipes. This can be a great help. However, if you examine them carefully before you cook, you may find that the fat content of some recipes is truly significant and that many low cholesterol recipes are still high in total fat.

It is not uncommon to find "company dishes" containing 40 to 60 grams of fat per serving! Many "regular family dinners" have 20 to 30 grams per serving. (Beware of SPARERIBS: 80 GRAMS PER SERVING — are they really that good?) Learn to read a recipe carefully and make changes or reject it if it has unacceptable amounts of fat.

Remember:

A 2000 calorie diet which is 20% fat will allow you 44 GRAMS OF FAT PER DAY.

A 2000 calorie diet which is 30% fat gives you 66 GRAMS OF FAT DAILY.

THE GOAL IS TO ELIMINATE FAT WHEN IT IS NOT NECESSARY AND SAVE YOUR FAT GRAMS FOR OTHER, MORE WORTHWHILE OCCASIONS!

One of the most practical pieces of knowledge you can have in choosing foods is on this page, so pay attention! It shows you how to convert grams of fat to calories and the way to calculate the percentage of fat calories in a food.

First you must remember there are 9 calories in each gram of fat.

To calculate the NUMBER OF FAT CALORIES, multiply the number of grams of fat by 9.

To calculate the PERCENTAGE OF FAT, divide the number of fat calories by the total calories.

EXAMPLE: 1 cup of skim milk contains 0.4 grams of fat and 90 calories.

0.4 grams of fat x 9 calories per gram = 3.6 fat calories

$$\frac{3.6 \text{ fat calories}}{90 \text{ Total calories}} \quad \text{x } 100\% = 4\% \text{ fat}$$

EXAMPLE: 1 cup of whole milk contains 9 grams of fat and 160 calories.

9 grams of fat x 9 calories per gram = 81 fat calories

$$\frac{81 \text{ fat calories}}{160 \text{ total calories}} \quad \text{x } 100\% = 50\% \text{ fat}$$

COOKING TIPS
TO SUPPORT YOUR NEW HABITS

Some of the more exciting experiences you will encounter in your new lowfat lifestyle will be different ways to prepare, cook and serve food. We have included many delicious recipes for eating the lowfat, high-fiber, fewer-empty-calories way and expect that you will find ways to adapt some of your own favorite recipes to fit this improved way of eating. We offer here some general tips on how to make changes in your cooking style which will save fat, calories and sugar.

KITCHEN ASSISTANTS: No lowfat kitchen should be without the following helpers:

A. A good set of NON-STICK COOKWARE (Silverstone coating is strongly recommended). If you don't own any, please buy at least a few pieces — the difference in fat requirements is amazing!

B. VEGETABLE COOKING SPRAY. Some people find it helpful to use a vegetable cooking spray if their non-stick cookware is no longer in perfect shape. We would be negligent if we didn't point out that many people have concerns about the safety of some of these products. They are sold in the form of aerosol sprays and, as such, have been abused as inhalants, with serious consequences. However, it is not clear whether any aerosol used in this manner would have had the same results or if the vegetable spray itself can be considered harmful.

C.   SHARP KNIVES. Invaluable for trimming fat from meat, removing chicken skin, cutting meat and cheese in T...H...I...N slices.

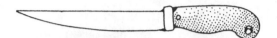

D.   KITCHEN SCALE. We don't believe in weighing everything you eat but a scale WILL help you to be aware of how much you are eating, especially if you're not used to gauging portion sizes accurately.

"FAT-FREE" MEAT COOKING: Of course no meat can be fat-free but you can cut out a great many unnecessary grams of fat (and calories) by choosing and cooking wisely.

Not all meat is riddled with fat. Lean cuts of meat do exist and they are as tasty as "the other brand". Flank steak and round steak are the best choices for beef — the first marinated, broiled and sliced very thin, the second browned in a scant amount of oil and slowly baked in a tasty sauce. There are endless variations on these themes, all delicious.

If you are a lamb fan (or want to become one), use the lean meat from a leg of lamb. It's not difficult to cut casserole-sized cubes from a lean leg of lamb (or the butcher may do it for you if you don't want to tackle it).

Start with a cold, non-stick skillet, sprayed with cooking spray (this latter is optional if your pan has a good non-stick surface). Heat meat slowly and it will brown in its own fat.

LOWFAT VERSUS NONFAT: Some recipes in this book use plain, lowfat yogurt. It is suggested primarily because it is easy to find, but you are encouraged to substitute nonfat yogurt. Do the same thing with milk — if you really can't force yourself to drink skim milk, at least use it in cooking where it doesn't make any difference in taste (but contributes significantly to a decrease in your total fat intake).

CHICKEN AND SKIN: The first time you remove the skin from four chicken breasts and heap it in a pile, we guarantee that you won't be nearly as interested in eating chicken skin as you thought you were! Removing the skin from breasts and thighs is easy to do — it peels away — and chicken without skin browns nicely in a very small amount of fat. For most chicken recipes in which the chicken pieces are simmered in some sort of sauce, it doesn't make any difference in taste whether or not the skin is on.

If you absolutely must have some skin on your chicken, at least brown the chicken skin-side down so it releases fat. Better yet, put it under the broiler for about 5 minutes and melt the fat out from under the skin.

UNRECOGNIZED HERO: Ground turkey! Have you tried it? Available in the frozen poultry section, it is very low in cost and relatively low in calories and fat. We have included several recipes using ground turkey, all of which can also be made with lean ground beef. (Remember that if you want to stick with beef, use the more expensive but less fatty LEAN ground beef.) Cut down on red meat consumption by giving turkey a try and feel good about your pocket book as well as your health.

COOKING A TURKEY: Remove most of the skin and use a foil tent to keep in moisture. Baste the turkey with chicken broth. Remember, our goal is fat-reduced, not fat-free.

BROWNING VEGETABLES: Most vegetables can be browned with almost no fat — even a Chinese-style stir-fry dinner for 4 can be accomplished with 1 — 2 teaspoons of oil. If the vegetables are to be browned only to be added to a soup, try leaving out that step entirely. There are times when a perfectly sauteed vegetable is a key ingredient of your meal. If the recipe features lightly browned mushrooms, you'll probably enjoy them more if you put a teaspoon of fat in the pan and watch them sizzle into brown morsels. That's OK!

Check some of your favorite recipes and see how many call for 2 — 4 tablespoons of fat for browning meat and vegetables. That's not browning, that's swimming! With few exceptions, you don't need the fat for flavor and with the improved non-stick pans you don't need it to avoid sticking.

BREADS: Many bread recipes call for up to ¼ cup of fat per loaf. A small amount of oil contributes to tender texture and adds some flavor, but changing the recipe to 1 tablespoon will accomplish that without affecting the end result.

To increase the fiber content of your diet, try substituting some whole grain cereal or flour for part of the all-purpose, white flour in your standard bread recipes. You may want to use at least 50% white flour, however, since most of the special grains and flours do not have adequate gluten. This protein substance makes the bread rise by stretching to form an elastic network which traps the gas bubbles formed by the yeast.

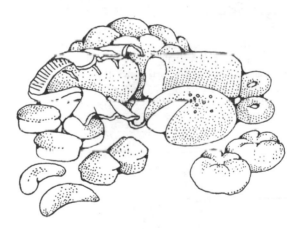

PANCAKES: Take your favorite pancake recipe and cut the oil first to ½ of the original amount, then try ½ of that the next time.

SWEET TREATS: In many cases you can cut down on sugar without disastrous results. Experiment with small changes at first — you may be pleasantly surprised.

CORNSTARCH: This is a staple in most cupboards that is used primarily to thicken calorie-laden fruit pies. However, it has great value in thickening sauces and casseroles as well. Its thickening power is greater than that of flour, it is much less inclined to lump and fat is not required when making a sauce (as opposed to flour-based sauces, which start with butter or margarine). Read the instructions on the package, but remember a few basics: 1 tablespoon of cornstarch thickens 1 — 2 cups of liquid; it must be mixed with a small amount of cold liquid first to make a smooth paste, then it can be added freely to the hot liquid. Boil it for 1 minute in order to remove any "starchy" taste and thicken properly.

Cornstarch mixed with skim milk may never replace heavy cream and an egg yolk for the final touch in French dishes, but you will find that it is surprisingly satisfactory for a great many recipes. Try it!

COOKING WITH HERBS

Decreasing fat from your diet should stimulate your imagination and challenge your creativity to find new ways to season your food without adding unnecessary calories.

Fresh herbs are notoriously overlooked in modern kitchens and can add a variety of taste sensations to food that otherwise might strike you as quite bland. Although the flavors of fresh herbs are more "alive" than dried, we have used primarily dried herbs in our recipes because they are more readily available. If you are using dried herbs, replace them often and store them in a cool, dark place.

GO EASY — especially at first. Use herbs subtly, adding just enough to heighten natural food flavors. Start with ¼ teaspoon of dried herbs to four servings. If substituting fresh herbs for dried, use 3 to 4 times as much. Drying concentrates the flavor.

Add herbs at the same time as salt and pepper to meats, vegetables, sauces and quick soups. When slow-cooking foods such as stews, adding a dash of herbs during the last half hour of cooking will enhance the aroma.

Improve the color and flavor of dried herbs by moistening them with a liquid, using two parts liquid to one part herbs. Suit the liquid to the dish you're preparing — lemon juice for salads, broths for meats. Add herbs to cold sauces early...allow them to stand overnight, if possible.

Herbs of any kind, when used judiciously, can make an ordinary dish simply fantastic!

BASIL

In addition to growing your own you can buy basil as a whole leaf or ground. It has a slightly minty taste. Basil is a natural for tomato and potato dishes and is a must in Italian foods. Add it to vegetables, soups, salads and all meats.

A scant half-teaspoon gives subtle flavor to beef stew. Perk up tomato aspic with a pinch of basil. Add it to tomato juice cocktail. Try it in hamburger patties. Lowfat cheese dishes sparkle with basil.

BAY LEAF

Bay leaves, a form of laurel, provide a pleasant aromatic taste to food whether they are whole or ground. They are a subtle herb, particularly suitable for soups or stews.

Add a bay leaf to the water when you cook potatoes for salad. Tomato sauces designed for fish are great with some bay leaf. Add one anytime you cook stew with vegetables. Try crushing the leaves and adding them to tomato aspic.

CHIVES

These are easy to grow in your kitchen garden. Use them fresh, frozen or dried. The flavor is mild and onion-like, good in lowfat cottage cheese, in egg dishes and in cream soups (made with lowfat milk, of course).

Chopped fresh chives on any light colored food create a pretty and flavorful garnish. Yogurt and chives make a saucy topper for baked potatoes. Add chopped chives to your spaghetti dishes.

DILL

Dill is a member of the parsley family, easily grown. Use either fresh or dried leaves, or whole or ground seeds. Delicious in fish, chicken and egg dishes. Dill and lemon are a perfect match.

Poach chicken breasts in dill-flavored water. Add to tuna salad for a piquant taste. Sprinkle some in your omelet mixture to add color.

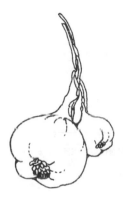

GARLIC/GARLIC POWDER

We're not purists — use whichever you prefer. About ¼ teaspoon powder is equal to one small clove of garlic. This is a zinger for meats, vegetables, salads and dressings.

Garlic gives zest to green salads. Pep up steaks with a sprinkle of garlic before broiling. Add it to tomato soup along with some sage. Try it with green beans.

MARJORAM

Another kitchen garden favorite, it's also available in ground form. This is a member of the mint family and has a spicy, pleasant aroma and taste. Marjoram is a classic with lamb and will accent mushrooms nicely.

A dash of marjoram in dressing goes well with green salads. It spices up tomato juice...seems to work with everything.

MINT

Mint is easy to grow and delightful in the garden. You can purchase it fresh or get the dried flakes in a can. The flavor is cool and refreshing. It's delicious with lamb, peas and carrots. Fruit beverages, fruit cups and salads are more delightful with the addition of mint.

Drop some fresh mint leaves in with peas as they simmer. Cooked carrots take to the flavor and color of dried mint.

OREGANO

Oregano is a good kitchen garden herb which can also be purchased whole or ground. It is a favorite with Italian and Mexican cooks. This herb gives character to meat, potatoes and tomatoes.

Sprinkle some oregano in potato or seafood salad. A dash of oregano is great with tomatoes. Pizza — the lowfat way — tastes great with oregano. Make a meat loaf taste Italian with oregano. It adds a zesty flavor to bean dishes and is mandatory with spaghetti!

PARSLEY

One of the most popular fresh garden herbs, parsley is also available dried or freeze-dried. The flavor is strong and distinctive and can be used with almost any food except sweet dishes.

Blend parsley into yogurt dips for vegetables. Add it in generous amounts to fish stews. Enjoy new potatoes, boiled and sauced lightly with lemon and parsley.

ROSEMARY

This is a potent herb, distinctively fresh with a hint of sweetness. It is a flavor complement to garlic and parsley.

Trying cauliflower? Add some rosemary. Combine it with chicken for a new and different taste.

ROSEMARY

SAGE

This herb has a strong flavor but it's an appetizing one. It blends well in soups and salads and is a must for turkey stuffing!

Add a dash of sage to tomato soup. Mix with lowfat cottage cheese for a delicious spread. Add it to clam chowder.

SAVORY

This comes as a whole leaf or ground. The flavor is piquant but subtle, good in stuffings, stews, meat balls, beans and peas.

Savory is wonderful with celery when making sauces. Sprinkle some in pea soup and on salad vegetables.

TARRAGON

Buy this as a whole leaf or ground. It's the perfect herb for all seafoods...hot or cold. Use it in chicken and tomato dishes or in sauces and salad dressings.

Tarragon gives a tang to lowfat tartar sauce. It makes lowfat cheese zesty.

THYME

Easily grown, thyme is also available as whole leaves or ground. This herb has a strong and distinctive aroma and blends well with other herbs. It is popular for seasoning soups and chowders. Use it with carrots, peas or onions.

Onion soup and a dash of thyme go together. For variety, sprinkle thyme on sliced tomatoes or salad greens.

THYME

NIBBLES and BITES

NIBBLES AND BITES

BLUE CHEESE DIP

   1 cup lowfat cottage cheese
   ¼ cup Whipped Cottage Cream Cheese, p. 171
   4 ounces crumbled blue cheese

Blend all ingredients together until smooth. Chill for 2 hours to develop flavor. Makes 2 cups. PER ¼ CUP: 90 CALORIES, 5 GRAMS FAT.

ONION DIP

   1 cup lowfat yogurt
   1 teaspoon onion salt
   1 teaspoon garlic salt
   1 teaspoon lemon juice

Stir together. Makes 1 cup. PER ¼ CUP: 40 CALORIES, 1 GRAM FAT.

RANCH DIP

   1 package dry ranch-style dressing mix
   1 cup lowfat yogurt
   1 tablespoon lowfat mayonnaise

Stir together. Makes 1 cup.

VEGETABLE SALAD PLATTER TO SERVE WITH DIPS

1 head cauliflower
1 pint cherry tomatoes
1 bunch broccoli (florets and short stems)
4 carrots
1 bunch green onions
3 stalks celery
8 ounce can button mushrooms
8 ounce jar artichoke hearts
8 ounce bottle low-calorie Italian dressing

Cut all vegetables into bite-size pieces, except tomatoes. Put all into large, heavy plastic bag, pour dressing into bag and mix well. Marinate overnight in refrigerator, turning often. Drain thoroughly and serve in large glass bowl or on fancy platter.

Mound these spreads in a bowl and surround with small squares of pumpernickel bread or cocktail rye rounds.

DILLED SHRIMP SPREAD

1 cup cooked shrimp (or water-packed tuna)
½ cup chopped celery
2 tablespoons chopped green onion
1 teaspoon dried dill
1 tablespoon lemon juice
2 tablespoons Mock Sour Cream, p. 170
2 tablespoons lowfat mayonnaise
  salt and pepper to taste

Chop shrimp, add celery and onion and mix with remaining ingredients or mix everything in food processor with short bursts until well blended. Chill well. Makes 1½ cups. PER ¼ CUP: 50 CALORIES, 2 GRAMS FAT.

CURRIED CHICKEN SPREAD

1 cup poached chicken (no skin)
2 tablespoons chopped green onion
¼ cup chopped celery
1 teaspoon curry powder
2 tablespoons Mock Sour Cream, p. 170
2 tablespoons lowfat mayonnaise
¼ teaspoon salt
1 teaspoon lemon juice
2 tablespoons toasted almonds

Dice chicken finely, add all other ingredients and mix well. If desired, blend in food processor for smooth paste but in this case leave out almonds and add them after blending. Chill well. Makes 1½ cups. PER ¼ CUP: 50 CALORIES, 3 GRAMS FAT.

DEVILLED TURKEY HAM SPREAD

    1 cup ground turkey ham (4 ounces)
    ⅓ cup chopped celery
    2 tablespoons pickle relish
    ½ teaspoon Dijon mustard
    ½ teaspoon horseradish sauce
    3 tablespoons Mock Sour Cream, p. 170
    2 tablespoons lowfat mayonnaise

Mix all ingredients together. Chill well. Makes 1½ cups. PER ¼ CUP: 50 CALORIES, 3 GRAMS FAT.

NOTE: The devilled turkey ham spread is outstanding as a celery stuffer! Any of these can also be used as a sandwich spread.

PARSLEY

Parsley adds color to almost every dish. Store it by rinsing well and shaking off the excess water. Then wrap in several thicknesses of damp paper towels. Keep in a sealed plastic bag in the refrigerator. Better yet, grow your own and have it fresh all the time!

The following recipe makes a large quantity of scrumptious spread - only the olives add any fat to speak of, so if you're really being strict you can cut down on them. All other amounts are fairly flexible - don't worry about getting the exact size can listed here. Measurements are approximate and you can make substitutions easily. This freezes very well and makes any cracker a standout!

SPICY SHRIMP MIX

   3 ounces black olives (about 12 large)
   4 ounce can of mushroom stems and pieces
   5 ounce jar of pickled onions
   2 ounce can of rolled anchovies
   3 ounce can albacore tuna packed in water
   ½ cup cooked tiny shrimp
   1 pickled HOT jalapeno pepper
  12 ounces catsup

Mix all ingredients except catsup and chop finely (or put quickly through food processor - you do not want a puree but a slightly chunky yet spreadable mixture). Place chopped mixture in saucepan and add catsup. Simmer 10 minutes, stirring often.

Place mixture in glass bowl, cover tightly and marinate for 2-3 days before using or freezing. Makes 3 cups. PER ¼ CUP: 70 CALORIES, 3 GRAMS FAT.

NOTE: The pickled pepper is an important ingredient, but it's your decision as to how hot you want the mixture. We like things spicy and found that one hot pepper, about 3 inches long, was plenty. If you like it hotter, add some of the pickling juices.

This is not fat free since it's hard to take the skin off chicken wings, but it's a big hit with everyone and worth it occasionally!

CHINESE CHICKEN WINGS

    24 ounces beer
    24 ounces soy sauce
    48 chicken wings, "drumstick" piece only
        sesame seeds

Mix together beer and soy sauce, pour over chicken wings and marinate for 24 hours in large baking dish. Bake at 325 degrees for 1 hour until chicken wings are very tender. Remove from oven, sprinkle with sesame seeds and place on cocktail table along with lots of napkins!

QUICHE QUBES

    ¾ cup grated part-skim mozzarella cheese
    ¾ cup grated cheddar cheese
    ½ teaspoon salt
    ½ teaspoon dried basil
    2 ounces diced turkey ham
    2 eggs + 1 egg white
    1 cup skim milk

Use a 1 quart baking dish sprayed with non-stick cooking spray. Sprinkle grated cheeses, salt, basil and turkey ham into the dish and stir gently to mix.

Beat together eggs, egg white and milk and pour over the mixture in the pan, stirring until everything is well mixed. Bake at 350 degrees for 45 minutes or until cheese is firmly set. Serve hot or cold. Makes about 30 pieces. PER PIECE: 30 CALORIES, 2 GRAMS FAT.

SHRIMP WON TONS

½ pound cooked tiny shrimp
4 ounces chopped water chestnuts
¼ cup chopped green onion
1 tablespoon soy sauce
1 tablespoon sherry
1 teaspoon cornstarch
⅛ teaspoon ground ginger
24 won ton wrappers
1 teaspoon oil
¼ cup water
1 tablespoon soy sauce
2 tablespoons white vinegar

Mix together shrimp, water chestnuts, green onion, soy sauce, sherry, cornstarch and ginger. Rather than chopping everything separately, you can place the ingredients in a food processor and chop finely with a few short bursts. The final result should be much like a paste.

To assemble the won tons, set out half a dozen wrappers at a time (they will dry out quickly), place 1 teaspoon of filling on each, moisten edges of dough with water and pinch together in a triangular shape. Set them upright on a baking sheet - they will look like tiny paper hats. When all are made, they can be frozen on this sheet then tossed into plastic bags until you need them. When ready to use, remove won tons from freezer but don't thaw!

For 24 won tons, heat 1 teaspoon oil in large non-stick frying pan, add won tons, flat bottom down. Cook uncovered for about 5 minutes or until bottoms are golden brown. Then pour in ¼ cup water, reduce heat, cover and steam 5 minutes. Serve hot with a mixture of soy sauce and white vinegar for dipping. Makes 24.

BEEF WON TONS

6 ounces lean ground beef
2 cups very finely chopped green cabbage
3 tablespoons chopped green onion
2 tablespoons oyster sauce
dash garlic powder
⅛ teaspoon dried ginger

Mix all ingredients together. Fill and cook won tons according to previous instructions.

You can't find a simpler treat than this one - plus it takes a while to eat and provides fiber.

MARINATED ARTICHOKE

1 large fresh artichoke
2 tablespoons lowfat Italian dressing
2 tablespoons lowfat mayonnaise
2 tablespoons lowfat yogurt
1 teaspoon lemon juice

Trim spiky tops of artichoke leaves with a sharp knife and cut off the stem at the bottom. Set artichoke upright in a saucepan containing 1 inch of water. Spread leaves slightly and pour Italian dressing INTO the artichoke. Cover pan and simmer for 30 minutes; turn artichoke upside-down and continue cooking for another 30 minutes. When heart can be pierced easily by a fork and tough bottom leaves snap off easily, the artichoke is done. Remove from water and let cool. Spread the leaves open to form a wide cup shape and scrape out the center fuzzy choke. Mix together mayonnaise, yogurt and lemon juice and fill the center of the artichoke with this mixture for dipping. Serves two. PER SERVING: 90 CALORIES, 6 GRAMS FAT.

POTATO SKINS

    3 large potatoes, about 4 inches long
    1 teaspoon margarine
    1 teaspoon oil
      salt and pepper
      toppings (see next page)

Bake potatoes until done. Cool and cut a lengthwise slice, ¼ inch thick at edges, from one side, then turn and repeat on the other 3 sides of each potato, for a total of 12 pieces. Centers will have extra potato pulp which can be scooped out after slicing to make skins of even thickness. (This much can be done ahead and skins can be set aside, tightly covered, until ready to top.)

Cut each skin in half to make a total of 24 pieces. Stir-fry skins in a mixture of margarine and oil until hot and crusty. Sprinkle with salt and pepper and add desired topping.

Each topping recipe makes enough to top 24 pieces.

NOTE: Calorie and gram counts do not include the potato skins since nutritional data is not available. However, a whole potato has about 140 calories and essentially no fat, therefore the skins alone have to be significantly less. The skins are filling and this recipe will easily satisfy four people for pre-dinner nibblings.

SOUR CREAM AND CHIVE TOPPING

½ cup Mock Sour Cream, p. 170
¼ cup chopped fresh chives

Spread mock sour cream on hot skins, top with chives, serve at once. PER 6 SKINS: 35 CALORIES, 1.7 GRAMS FAT.

HAM 'N CHEESE TOPPING

3 ounces diced turkey ham
¾ cup grated part-skim mozzarella cheese

Sprinkle ham and cheese on skins, slip under broiler just until cheese melts. Serve at once. PER 6 SKINS: 65 CALORIES, 4.2 GRAMS FAT.

TOMATO PIZZA TOPPING

¼ cup tomato sauce
⅛ teaspoon dried oregano
½ cup grated cheddar cheese

Spread tomato sauce on skins, sprinkle oregano over sauce and top with grated cheese. Broil just until cheese melts. Serve at once. PER 6 SKINS: 55 CALORIES, 4.3 GRAMS FAT.

STUFFED MUSHROOMS

18 large fresh mushrooms
1 teaspoon oil
¼ cup finely chopped onion
¼ pound lean ground beef
2 teaspoons Worcestershire sauce
1 teaspoon garlic powder
½ teaspoon salt
¼ cup grated cheddar cheese

Remove stems from mushrooms and chop finely. Set aside. Heat oil in a large skillet, cook onion and ground beef until lightly browned. Break up beef chunks until mixture is very fine, otherwise the stuffing tends to fall out of the mushrooms! Add the chopped mushroom stems, Worcestershire sauce, garlic powder and salt to onion-beef mixture and cook five minutes.

Stuff mixture into mushroom caps, sprinkle with cheese. This much can be done ahead and mushrooms set on broiler pan. Just before serving, preheat broiler and broil caps about 3-4 minutes. Serve hot with lots of napkins! EACH: 35 CALORIES, 2 GRAMS FAT.

HAM-PINEAPPLE TIDBITS

The secret here is to use lowfat turkey ham. Just cut equal amounts of turkey ham and pineapple (fresh or packed in its own juice) into small cubes. Place one cube of each on a toothpick and set out for easy munching.

TURKEY MINIMEATBALLS

1 pound lean ground turkey
½ cup crushed cracker crumbs
¼ cup finely chopped onion
1 slightly beaten egg
1 tablespoon chicken broth (or water)
1 tablespoon Worcestershire sauce
½ teaspoon salt
½ teaspoon poultry seasoning

Mix together all ingredients and form into small, bite-size balls. Place meatballs on top of broiler pan so any fat will drip away. Bake at 375 degrees for 20 minutes or until brown. Meanwhile, prepare either sauce. Makes 60.

SPICY COCKTAIL SAUCE

¼ cup chile sauce
1 tablespoon vinegar
1 tablespoon brown sugar

Mix all ingredients together, use as a dipping sauce. PER 5 MEATBALLS: 115 CALORIES, 6 GRAMS FAT.

CREAMY DILL SAUCE

1 tablespoon cornstarch
1 cup chicken broth
½ teaspoon dried dill
½ cup lowfat yogurt
    salt to taste

Blend cornstarch with small amount of broth until smooth, then add to rest of broth and bring to boil. Add dill and yogurt. Add meatballs to the sauce and simmer briefly to blend flavors. Keep warm in chafing dish. PER 5 MEATBALLS: 125 CALORIES, 6 GRAMS FAT.

EASY NO-COOK CANAPES

Use fresh fruit instead of a platter of raw vegetables. Cut pear, peach, pineapple, nectarine, apple or melon into bite-size pieces. Dip fruit into water containing several tablespoons of lemon juice to prevent the fruit from darkening.

Arrange on a platter around a bowl of FRUIT DIP. Blend one cup of lowfat yogurt with some fruit juice or sugar substitute and squirt in some lemon juice. Add drained, crushed pineapple to taste.

One of the easiest and most enjoyable canapes is FROZEN GRAPES - freeze and serve JUST before they are to be eaten - they don't look too terrific if they melt again!

SOUP'S ON

SOUP'S ON

Add a tossed salad and French bread for a complete, low cost, high fiber, nourishing meal!

RIB-STICKER SOUP

¼ cup dried white navy beans
¼ cup dried small red beans
¼ cup dried yellow split peas
¼ cup dried green split peas
¼ cup dried lentils
1 large chopped onion
2 cups chopped celery
1 clove crushed garlic
½ teaspoon salt
1 tablespoon dried basil
1 tablespoon Worcestershire sauce
2 cups tomato sauce
2 cups stewed tomatoes
4 cups beef broth

Soak dried beans, peas and lentils overnight in water to cover. Add all other ingredients the next day, stir to mix well. Bring to boiling, then lower heat, cover and simmer 3-4 hours or until vegetables are very tender. If soup is too thick, additional broth or water can be added without changing the final flavor. Serves 8. PER SERVING: 150 CALORIES, LESS THAN 1 GRAM FAT.

Here's a simple vegetable soup to make in the middle of winter, using fresh vegetables - the color will perk you up!

WINTER VEGETABLE SOUP

2 cups beef broth
½ cup diced carrot
½ cup chopped celery
1 small diced potato, about 1 cup
1 cup stewed tomatoes
¼ teaspoon dried basil
½ teaspoon salt, to taste
¼ cup chopped green onion
1 cup chopped fresh spinach

Combine all ingredients, except onion and spinach, in large pot. Simmer until vegetables are tender (about 25 minutes). Add onion and spinach, heat 5 minutes. Serves 3. PER SERVING: 80 CALORIES, LESS THAN 1 GRAM FAT.

SALT AND SOUP

Beef and chicken broths used in making soups have wide variations in salt content so be cautious when adding additional salt. Most recipes will suggest that you "salt to taste".

You will notice that many of our recipes call for beef or chicken broth. You can buy a good brand of bouillon and keep it in your pantry but we recommend home-made chicken and beef broths as soup bases - you know they are almost fat-free and they tend to be less salty than the commercial varieties.

Making your own broth is not difficult and it's a very satisfying thing to do. Follow the recipes below as a general guide.

Measurements are, of necessity, approximate. (Who's going to measure bones?) Basically, you accumulate bones in your freezer, then simmer them with whatever vegetables you have around (fresh or frozen) and season to taste.

This broth has so many uses that once you try making it you'll probably decide that you should always have it on hand in your freezer.

HOMEMADE BEEF OR CHICKEN BROTH

Enough bones to fill 8 quart pot
2 cups chopped celery, plus leaves
2 chopped carrots
2 chopped onions
½ teaspoon dried oregano
½ teaspoon dried thyme
2 bay leaves
4 cloves garlic
1 tablespoon salt, to start

BEEF BROTH: Brown the bones under the broiler first and save juices; place in pot, add vegetables and spices. Cover bones with water, bring to a boil, cover pot and simmer 2-6 hours. You can't overcook this! Strain the broth into another large pot, leaving behind the bones and vegetables, which by now will be looking rather tired.

Remove the bones, cool and check for meat. Discard bones and vegetables. Chill the stock overnight and remove the layer of fat which will have solidified on the top.

Reheat the stock, adjust seasoning, continue simmering if you want it more concentrated. When done to your liking, ladle into freezer containers and freeze. This amount makes 6-8 pints. Almost no calories (about 25/cup), essentially no fat.

CHICKEN BROTH: Don't brown the bones first, otherwise follow the above recipe. Cooked or uncooked bones are fine. If using all cooked bones, simmering 2-3 hours is sufficient.

OLD-FASHIONED CHICKEN SOUP

> 4 cups chicken broth
> cooked chicken bits, if available
> 2 sliced carrots
> 4 sliced celery stalks
> ½ teaspoon dried dill
> 2 ounces thin noodles, broken up

Heat chicken broth to boiling, add vegetables and dill, cover and simmer for 15 minutes or until barely tender. Add noodles and simmer 10 minutes or until tender. Adjust salt. Serves 4. PER SERVING: 75 CALORIES, LESS THAN 1 GRAM FAT.

Another heart-warming, comforting variation of mama's chicken soup.

BARLEY SOUP

4 cups chicken broth
½ cup pearl barley
¼ teaspoon dried basil
½ cup chopped celery
½ cup chopped carrots
1 cup chopped mushrooms

Simmer broth, barley, basil, celery and carrots together until barley is tender, about 1 hour. Add mushrooms and simmer 15 more minutes. Adjust salt. Serves 4. PER SERVING: 100 CALORIES, LESS THAN 1 GRAM FAT.

PUREED PEA SOUP

¼ cup green split peas
¼ cup yellow split peas
½ cup chopped onion
1½ cups beef broth
1½ cups water
1 teaspoon salt

Soak peas overnight in 1 quart of water. Drain, rinse and place in 2 quart pot. Add all other ingredients and simmer until peas are tender, about 2 hours. Blend until smooth in food processor or blender. Serves 4. PER SERVING: 95 CALORIES, LESS THAN 1 GRAM FAT.

This soup freezes well, providing a "taste of summer" during dark winter days, and it is very inexpensive to make when all these vegetables are in season.

GARDEN FRESH VEGETABLE SOUP

1 cup sliced carrots
1 cup sliced celery
1 cup chopped onion
1 clove crushed garlic
4 cups chopped fresh tomatoes
2 cups beef broth
½ teaspoon dried basil
½ teaspoon dried thyme
½ teaspoon salt
1 cup fresh green beans, in 1 inch lengths
2 cups sliced zucchini

Mix together all ingredients except zucchini in a 4 quart saucepan. Bring to a boil, then cover and simmer 30 minutes. Add zucchini and simmer 15 minutes more. Serves 6. PER SERVING: 80 CALORIES, 2 GRAMS FAT.

Serve with tossed salad and wine for a fantastic meal.

FRENCH ONION SOUP

> 6 large, thinly sliced onions
> 1 tablespoon olive oil
> 6 cups beef broth
>   salt and pepper to taste
> ⅓ cup red port wine (or white wine)
> ½ cup diced lowfat Gruyere cheese
>   toasted whole wheat bread
> 6 tablespoons grated Parmesan cheese

In a heavy-bottomed 4 quart saucepan, brown onions in oil until limp and golden. Cover and simmer slowly for 15 minutes. Pour in beef broth and simmer for 30 minutes. Add salt and pepper to taste.

Pour soup and wine into ovenproof tureen or casserole, cover and heat in a 350 degree oven for 30 minutes. Remove from oven and increase heat to 425 degrees.

Pour soup into individual ovenproof bowls. Sprinkle with diced Gruyere cheese. Cover with a layer of toasted bread and sprinkle Parmesan cheese over the top. Serves 6. PER SERVING: 200 CALORIES, 7 GRAMS FAT.

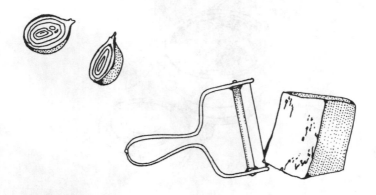

TOMATO-LENTIL SOUP

    1 cup lentils
    3 cups cold water
    1 teaspoon oil
    1 chopped onion
    1 clove minced garlic
    ½ cup chopped celery
    2 cups chopped tomatoes (fresh or canned)
    ½ teaspoon salt
    6 cups beef broth
    1 large potato, cut in ½ inch cubes

Place lentils and 3 cups water in pan, bring to boil, then cover and simmer 1 hour. Do NOT drain! Heat oil, add onion, garlic and celery, simmer 5 minutes. Add to lentils in water, along with tomatoes, salt and beef broth. Simmer 2 hours. Add potato, simmer an additional 30 minutes. Adjust salt. Serves 10. PER SERVING: 125 CALORIES, 2 GRAMS FAT.

NOTE: This soup freezes well and tastes even better when thawed!

FAT FREE SAUCES

Plan ahead so you can chill your soup thoroughly before eating - all fat will rise to the surface and can then be lifted out in a solid block. Then reheat and enjoy. Thick and hearty soups always seem better anyway when made 24 hours before eating so that flavors can blend.

CREAM OF ASPARAGUS SOUP

    4 cups chicken broth
    2 cups chopped fresh asparagus
    4 tablespoons chopped onion
    1 cup lowfat yogurt

Heat chicken broth and cook asparagus and onion until soft. Cool slightly and blend until smooth. Add yogurt and reheat gently. Serve at once. Serves 4. PER SERVING: 100 CALORIES, 1.5 GRAMS FAT.

Four chilled soups for warm summer days!

CUCUMBER/SPINACH SOUP

    3 cups chicken broth
    2 medium cucumbers (about 2 cups)
    1 chopped onion
      salt to taste
    1 clove minced garlic
    1 cup chopped fresh spinach
    1 cup lowfat yogurt

Place chicken broth in 4 quart saucepan. Peel, seed and chop cucumbers and add to broth along with onion, salt and garlic. Bring to a boil, simmer about 30 minutes or until vegetables are soft. Add chopped spinach and cook 5 minutes more.

In small batches, puree mixture in food processor or blender. CAUTION: hot liquid may spurt out of blending container - let cool slightly and use small batches. Add yogurt to vegetable mixture and blend all.

Refrigerate soup until very cold. Shake well before serving in chilled bowls. Serves 6. PER SERVING: 50 CALORIES, 1 GRAM FAT.

CREAMY COLD ZUCCHINI SOUP

2 cups chicken broth
3 cups sliced zucchini
2 chopped onions
1 clove minced garlic
¼ teaspoon curry powder
  salt to taste
1 cup lowfat yogurt
2 teaspoons lemon juice

Place broth, zucchini, onions, garlic, curry and salt in a saucepan and bring to a boil. Reduce heat to low, cover and simmer until vegetables are tender.

Cool. Blend vegetables until smooth and creamy. (See CAUTION on previous page.) Add yogurt and lemon juice. Chill until very cold and serve in chilled bowls. Serves 4. PER SERVING: 75 CALORIES, 1 GRAM FAT.

GAZPACHO

    1 cup tomato-vegetable juice
    1 large onion
    1 large green pepper
    2 medium zucchini
    2 large ripe tomatoes, peel removed
    1 clove minced garlic
    1 tablespoon olive oil
    2 tablespoons wine vinegar
    3 cups chicken broth
        salt and pepper to taste
        chopped vegetables for garnish

Place juice, vegetables and garlic in blender or food processor and process until coarsely chopped. Pour into a large bowl and whisk in oil, wine vinegar and chicken broth. Chill thoroughly.

When serving, pass small bowls of additional chopped vegetables if desired. Serves 4.

NOTE: Soup can be frozen, then processed to a slush consistency.

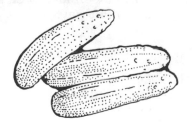

ANOTHER GAZPACHO!

1 large tomato, peel removed
1 large cucumber, peeled and seeded
1 medium onion
1 green pepper
1 46 oz. can tomato-vegetable juice
1 clove minced garlic
2 tablespoons olive oil
⅓ cup wine vinegar
¼ teaspoon hot pepper sauce
1 teaspoon salt (more to taste)
¼ teaspoon coarse black pepper
¼ cup chopped chives
   croutons

In blender, combine ½ tomato, ½ cucumber, ½ onion, ¼ green pepper, ½ cup juice and garlic. Blend 30 seconds. In a large bowl or pitcher combine the pureed vegetables and remaining juice, oil, vinegar and seasonings.

Chop the unblended remaining ingredients and place in small bowls to pass as garnish for soup. Chill all for at least 2 hours and serve in chilled bowls. Serves 6-8.

NOTE: You can puree all the vegetables instead of reserving some for garnish, if you prefer a smoother soup.

Try this with some dark pumpernickel bread for a healthy and delicious treat on a rainy day.

BORSCHT

½ cup chopped onion
1 16 ounce can sliced beets, plus juice
2 cups shredded cabbage
½ cup chopped carrot
½ cup diced potato
2 tablespoons vinegar
4 cups beef stock
¼ cup lowfat yogurt

Combine all ingredients except yogurt and simmer for 1 hour or until vegetables are tender. Cool slightly, then blend small amounts carefully in blender. Return blended mixture to pot and heat through. Serve in wide bowls with 1 tablespoon of yogurt in center of each serving. Serves 4. PER SERVING: 110 CALORIES, LESS THAN 1 GRAM FAT.

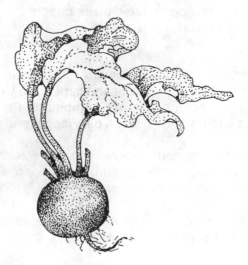

MAIN DISH MEATS

MAIN DISH MEATS

ABOUT PROTEINS

Our bodies use protein to build muscle tissue, help in blood clotting, manufacture enzymes and hormones and provide antibodies to fight infection. They keep our bodies healthy by providing the essential amino acids (supplied from external body sources) and enough chemical components to allow the body to make the nonessential amino acids. They should be remembered as the "building blocks" of the body.

When the body is deprived of calories (as in low calorie dieting), it begins to conserve fat and calls on protein tissue (muscles) as an energy source. Very strict diets can actually destroy your muscles. It is very important to maintain healthy levels of lean body protein tissue. Not only are these the tissues that burn the most calories, they are essential to maintenance of good health.

High protein foods include meats, legumes, fish, chicken, nuts and most dairy products.

Americans typically consume up to 40% of their diet as protein. This is much more than our bodies need, even when engaged in a very active lifestyle or a weight lifting program.

U.S. DIETARY GOALS RECOMMEND A DIET IN WHICH 12% OF THE CALORIES COME FROM PROTEIN SOURCES. The focus we have put on including protein-rich foods, in large amounts, at every meal, may be one of the places to look when evaluating how we choose foods. Although protein is an essential part of a balanced diet, small amounts of protein products can supply the nutrients we need for building new cells and tissues and maintaining those already present.

ORIENTAL FLANK STEAK

1 pound flank steak
2 tablespoons soy sauce
2 teaspoons honey
¼ cup cider vinegar
¼ teaspoon hot pepper sauce
¼ teaspoon garlic powder

Mix marinade ingredients well, pour over flank steak placed in plastic bag. Let stand 4-24 hours in the refrigerator, turning often to distribute marinade. When ready to cook, remove from marinade and place over hot coals or broil until done to your liking. Serves 4. PER SERVING: 180 CALORIES, 5 GRAMS FAT.

NOTE: This steak is best served rare or medium-rare and sliced very thinly across the grain.

BARBECUED FLANK STEAK

1 pound flank steak
¼ cup wine vinegar
½ teaspoon onion powder
2 tablespoons Worcestershire sauce
½ teaspoon dried thyme
¼ teaspoon garlic powder
⅛ teaspoon hot pepper sauce

Shake all marinade ingredients together very well, follow directions above. Serves 4. PER SERVING: 180 CALORIES, 5 GRAMS FAT.

STUFFED FLANK STEAK

2 tablespoons margarine
¼ cup chopped onion
¼ teaspoon dried thyme
2 cups coarse fresh bread crumbs
1 pound flank steak
2 tablespoons Worcestershire sauce
1 cup red wine
1 cup beef broth

Heat margarine and cook onion until soft; sprinkle thyme over bread crumbs, add onion/margarine mixture and toss with a fork until well mixed. Butterfly the flank steak by slitting it horizontally with a very sharp knife. Cut within ½ inch of one edge so the steak can be spread open like a book to become twice the original size and half the thickness.

Spread stuffing over steak and roll up carefully, using toothpicks to keep steak edges together. Brown the meat in a non-stick pan. Mix together Worcestershire sauce, wine and broth, pour over meat, cover pan and simmer for about 1 hour or until meat is tender. Serves 4. PER SERVING: 350 CALORIES, 12 GRAMS FAT.

A standard "easy pot roast" recipe used to call for the cook to heat ¼ cup oil, brown meat thoroughly, brown some onions, pour a can of cream of mushroom soup over everything and bake until tender. Of course, all the fat was left in the pan! Look over some of your old favorite recipes - many of them read like this! Now we recommend browning meat in a scant amount of oil, adding onions and carrots and topping with beef broth - what a difference in fat!

APPLE POT ROAST

      2 pounds lean boneless meat
      1 teaspoon oil
      6 small onions
      5 carrots, cut in thirds
      ½ cup sliced celery
      1 bay leaf
      1 teaspoon salt or to taste
      1 cup apple juice
      1 cup beef broth or wine

Heat oil in Dutch oven. Add beef, brown well on all
sides. Add remaining ingredients, cover and place in a
300 degree oven for 1½-2 hours or until tender. Serves
8. PER SERVING: 270 CALORIES, 9 GRAMS FAT.

*This is a great recipe for a busy day - no stirring or
fussing required. Teach everyone in your family how to
throw this meal together!*

CHILE SWISS STEAK

      1 pound lean round steak, 1 inch thick
        flour
      1 teaspoon oil
    1½ cups beer (12 ounce can)
      1 cup bottled chile sauce
      1 tablespoon Worcestershire sauce

Press flour into both sides of the meat and pound with
edge of plate or mallet. Heat oil, brown the meat well,
pour over it the beer, chile sauce and Worcestershire
sauce. Cover and bake at 300 degrees for 1½ hours -
that's all! Serves 4. PER SERVING: 325 CALORIES,
10 GRAMS FAT.

LAZY DAY SWISS STEAK

1 pound lean round steak, 1 inch thick
  flour
1 teaspoon oil
1 quartered onion
4 small carrots, cut in 2 inch lengths
1 cup stewed tomatoes
1 tablespoon Worcestershire sauce
1 teaspoon salt
1 clove crushed garlic
1 bay leaf

Press flour into both sides of the meat, pound with edge of plate or mallet. Heat oil in non-stick frying pan and brown meat well. Add onion, carrots, tomatoes, Worcestershire sauce, salt, garlic and bay leaf. Cover and bake at 300 degrees for 1½ hours. Serves 4. PER SERVING: 260 CALORIES, 9 GRAMS FAT.

WEEKDAY/WORKDAY TIP

Oven-baked meals such as Apple Pot Roast, Chile Swiss Steak, Lazy Day Swiss Steak and Oven-Baked Stew can all be prepared ahead of time and placed in a covered casserole. If you have a self-timing oven, set it to start cooking one hour before you come home - or ask the first person home to put it in the oven. Last minute meal preparations such as a tossed salad can be made during the last half hour of cooking.

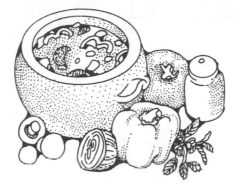

EASY OVEN-BAKED STEW

    1 pound lean beef, cut in 1 inch cubes
    2 medium onions
    2 large carrots
    4 celery stalks
    8 large mushrooms
    1 teaspoon oil
    1 teaspoon salt
  ⅛ teaspoon garlic powder
    1 bay leaf
    2 tablespoons Worcestershire sauce
    2 cups water

Brown beef in hot, non-stick skillet. Remove from pan. Cut onions in ¼'s, carrots and celery in 3-inch lengths and leave mushrooms whole. Add oil to skillet and brown vegetables briefly.

Arrange meat and vegetables in deep oven-proof casserole, sprinkle with salt and garlic powder; add bay leaf, Worcestershire sauce and water. Cover and bake at 300 degrees for 1½ hours or until very tender. More water may be added. Serves 4. PER SERVING: 300 CALORIES, 10 GRAMS FAT.

FAT TRICK

If you notice fat floating on the surface of your sauce as you are putting the final touches together, quickly dip an ice cube into the hot liquid. Excess fat will congeal on the surface.

BARBECUED BEEF

    2 pounds lean beef, cut 2 inches thick
    1 teaspoon oil
    1 cup chopped onion
    ½ cup white vinegar
    ¼ cup chile sauce
    ¼ cup tomato sauce
    2 teaspoons chile powder
    2 teaspoons Worcestershire sauce
    2 teaspoons sugar
    ¼ teaspoon thyme
    1 cup stewed tomatoes
    ½ cup beef broth
    ½ cup red wine

Cut meat into 2 inch square chunks. Brown in non-stick skillet, then remove and place in an oven-proof casserole dish. Heat oil in skillet, add onion and cook for 3 minutes. Add all other ingredients, bring to a boil, then pour over beef.

Cover and bake in a 300 degree oven for about 2½ hours or until meat falls apart in shreds when probed with a fork. Serve over toasted buns. Serves 8. PER SERVING: 280 CALORIES, 9 GRAMS FAT.

BEEF BURGUNDY

   1 pound lean round steak
     flour
   1 teaspoon oil
   1 clove minced garlic
 20 small pearl onions
  ½ teaspoon dried thyme
   1 bay leaf
   1 tablespoon Worcestershire sauce
   1 cup water
1½ cups red wine
   1 cup whole fresh mushrooms

Cut steak into 1 inch cubes. Pound flour into meat and brown in oil. Add garlic and onions and cook until lightly browned. Add all other ingredients except mushrooms, cover and simmer 1 hour. Add mushrooms and cook an additional ½ hour. Serves 4. PER SERVING: 320 CALORIES, 10 GRAMS FAT.

The way the beef is cut is important.

COMPETITION CHILI

    1 pound lean beef, coarsely chopped*
    1 cup chopped onion
    2 cloves crushed garlic
    2 tablespoons chili powder
    ¼ teaspoon hot pepper sauce
    1 tablespoon white vinegar
    1 teaspoon salt
    2 cups stewed tomatoes

*Buy the beef in a chunk, e.g. round steak, and dice it into ¼ inch cubes or chop briefly in the food processor. THIS IS IMPORTANT - it should not be finely ground. Cook meat in a deep non-stick pot until evenly browned. Add onion and garlic and cook for 5 minutes. Pour off any accumulated juices and fat.

Add all other ingredients. Bring mixture to a boil, then cover and simmer slowly for approximately 2 hours, or until thick. Serves 4. PER SERVING: 270 CALORIES, 9 GRAMS FAT.

NOTE: If you want to add beans to stretch the chili, be aware that adding 2 cups of canned kidney beans will add a total of 450 calories and 2 grams of fat. If it still serves 4, each serving will then have 380 calories and 9.5 grams fat.

BEEF SUKIYAKI

  1 pound thinly sliced top round steak
  1 teaspoon oil
  4 cups coarsely chopped bok choy or cabbage
  4 onions, cut in quarters
  4 sliced green onions
16 mushrooms
  4 cups chopped fresh spinach
  4 cups cooked Oriental cellophane noodles
    tofu
    whole almonds (optional)
  1 cup soy sauce
  1 cup water
  1 cup sake
  1 tablespoon sugar

Heat oil in large non-stick frying pan or wok (must have a cover). Place one layer of meat in pan and brown quickly on both sides - this provides some starting flavor for the mixture. Then begin layering vegetables into pan, adding a layer of uncooked meat after every inch of vegetables.

For example, over the browned meat place half of the bok choy, 8 onion quarters, half the sliced green onions and half the mushrooms, then place a layer of meat on this and continue with half the spinach, noodles, tofu and almonds, then another layer of meat. Repeat this layering if your pan can hold it, otherwise cook it in two batches.

Mix together soy sauce, water, sake and sugar and pour it over meat and vegetables (use all or half depending on amount of meat and vegetables used). Cover pan and steam sukiyaki until meat is cooked and vegetables are crunchy, 5-10 minutes. Serves 4.

BEEF 'N BROCCOLI

½ pound lean round steak, thinly sliced
2 tablespoons soy sauce
1 tablespoon dry sherry
2 tablespoons water
2 tablespoons cornstarch
1 teaspoon oil
½ cup sliced celery
¼ cup chopped onion
1 clove minced garlic
2 cups broccoli, florets and short stems
¼ cup water
2 tablespoons cornstarch

Marinate beef in a mixture of soy sauce, sherry, water and cornstarch for one hour at room temperature. When ready to serve, heat oil in large non-stick frying pan or wok until very hot. Brown celery, onion and garlic; remove beef from marinade (save the marinade) and brown quickly on both sides. Remove beef and vegetables and keep warm.

Add broccoli to frying pan along with ¼ cup water. Cover and steam just until fork tender.

Return beef and vegetables to pan; mix water and cornstarch, add to reserved marinade, shake well, pour into pan, cook and stir until thick. Serves 4. PER SERVING: 180 CALORIES, 5 GRAMS FAT.

A crusty loaf of bread to sop up juices makes a complete meal.

SHEPHERD'S SPRING LAMB STEW

1 pound lean boneless lamb
4 new potatoes
1 large sliced onion
2 cloves minced garlic
2 bay leaves
¼ teaspoon dried dill
1 teaspoon salt
1 cup chicken broth
1 cup white wine
1 cup peas, fresh or frozen
1 teaspoon cornstarch
1 teaspoon water

Cut lamb and potatoes into 1 inch cubes. Place in 1 quart stove-top casserole. Layer sliced onions and garlic over lamb and potatoes, add bay leaves, dill and salt.

Mix chicken broth and wine and pour over meat and vegetables. Cover, bring to a boil, reduce heat and simmer about 1 hour or until lamb is tender and potatoes are cooked.

10 minutes before serving, add peas and cook until tender. Remove meat and vegetables to serving bowl and keep warm; mix cornstarch and water, add to juices and boil quickly until thick. Pour over meat and vegetables. Serves 4. PER SERVING: 365 CALORIES, 8 GRAMS FAT.

NOTE: Best to serve this in bowls or au gratin dishes and eat with a spoon.

LEMON LAMB

1 pound lean boneless lamb
1 sliced onion
1 clove crushed garlic
½ teaspoon dried oregano
1 cup chicken broth
½ cup white wine
2 cups thinly sliced zucchini
1 teaspoon cornstarch
2 tablespoons lemon juice

Cut lamb into 1 inch cubes. Starting with cold, non-stick frying pan, heat lamb slowly on all sides until lightly browned. Stir in onion and garlic and brown lightly. Add oregano, broth and wine. Bring to boiling, then cover and simmer for 30-40 minutes or until meat is tender.

Add zucchini, cover and simmer 5 minutes more. Remove meat and vegetables from liquid and keep warm. Shake together cornstarch and lemon juice. Pour into pan and bring to a boil; cook and stir until thick and smooth. Season with salt to taste, then pour over reserved meat and vegetables. Serves 4. PER SERVING: 250 CALORIES, 8 GRAMS FAT.

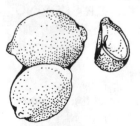

MOROCCAN LAMB

1 pound lean boneless lamb
1 teaspoon oil
½ cup mushrooms
½ cup chopped onion
¼ cup slivered almonds
½ cup raisins
2 cups stewed tomatoes
1 teaspoon sugar
1 teaspoon salt
½ teaspoon cinnamon
¼ teaspoon allspice
¼ teaspoon cloves
2 teaspoons lemon juice
1 teaspoon cornstarch

Cut lamb into 1 inch cubes. Starting with cold, non-stick frying pan, brown meat slowly on all sides. Remove from pan. Heat oil, add mushrooms and onions. Brown briefly. Stir in raisins, tomatoes and all spices and simmer for 5 minutes. Add lamb, bring to a boil, cover and simmer for 1 hour.

Mix together lemon juice and cornstarch, stir into liquid, boil for 1 minute. Serves 4. PER SERVING: 300 CALORIES, 9 GRAMS FAT.

DILLY TOMATO-LAMB STEW

1 pound lean boneless lamb
1 teaspoon oil
½ cup chopped onion
2 cups stewed tomatoes
½ cup white wine
½ teaspoon dried dill
1 teaspoon salt
1 tablespoon cornstarch
1 tablespoon water
¼ cup lowfat yogurt (optional)

Cut lamb into 1 inch cubes. Brown lamb in hot, non-stick skillet, then remove to stove-top saucepan. Heat oil in skillet, add onion and cook for 3 minutes. Add tomatoes, wine, dill and salt to onion, bring to a boil, then pour over lamb and simmer for 1½ hours or until lamb is tender.

Mix cornstarch and water together and add to sauce, bring sauce to a boil and cook until thick. For lovers of the stroganoff taste, add yogurt and cook gently until heated through. Pour sauce over lamb. Serves 4. PER SERVING: 265 CALORIES, 8 GRAMS FAT.

DILL

"Blanquette" is a French word for "white stew"- meaning no browning in fat before you start! It is classically made with veal but we find that tender leg of lamb cubes do just as well.

LAMB BLANQUETTE

1 pound lean boneless lamb
1 thinly sliced onion
¼ teaspoon dried thyme
1 clove minced garlic
½ teaspoon salt
2 cups beef broth
¼ cup white wine
1 carrot
1 celery stalk
16 frozen small pearl onions
¼ pound small button mushrooms
1 teaspoon oil
1 teaspoon cornstarch
1 tablespoon water
¼ cup lowfat yogurt
2 teaspoons lemon juice

Cut lamb into 1 inch cubes. Place cubed meat in large pan, cover and heat slowly so it simmers in its own juices for about 20 minutes. Add onion, thyme, garlic, salt, broth, wine, carrot and celery. Simmer 20 minutes, add small whole onions and simmer an additional 20 minutes.

Meanwhile, brown the mushrooms lightly in oil. Add to meat mixture a few minutes before end of cooking. Strain the stew through a colander, saving all juices. Arrange meat and vegetables on a serving dish and keep warm. Meanwhile, mix together cornstarch and water. Thicken broth with this paste by bringing to a boil for 2 minutes, or until thick and smooth. Add yogurt and lemon juice to taste; simmer gently until well blended. Serves 4. PER SERVING: 310 CALORIES, 9 GRAMS FAT.

QUICK LAMB CURRY FOR TWO

½ pound lean boneless lamb
1 teaspoon oil
¼ cup chopped onion
1-3 teaspoons curry powder
¼ teaspoon garlic powder
1 cup chicken broth
1 teaspoon cornstarch
1 teaspoon water
   frozen tiny green peas, barely cooked
   brown rice
   yogurt
   chutney
   green pepper jelly
   chopped tomatoes
   chopped cucumbers
   coconut

Cut lamb into 1 inch cubes. Starting with cold, non-stick frying pan, brown meat slowly on all sides. Add oil, brown onion slowly. Stir in curry powder and garlic powder and simmer 1 minute. Add chicken broth, bring to a boil, reduce heat and simmer for 30 minutes or until tender. If sauce has not thickened to your liking, blend in cornstarch and water mixture and cook 1 minute.

Thaw peas quickly by immersing in hot water.

Serve curry over a plate of hot brown rice, surrounded with a ring of peas. Pass condiments in separate small dishes. Serves 2. PER SERVING (curry only): 315 CALORIES, 10 GRAMS FAT.

NOTE: The amount of curry is optional and depends on your own taste buds and the quality of your curry powder. As a rule of thumb, usually 1 teaspoon = mild, 2 teaspoons = medium, 3 teaspoons (1 tablespoon) = HOT.

THAT'S SOME MEATBALL!

THAT'S SOME MEATBALL!

All of the recipes which follow can, of course, be made with any lean ground meat. Most of us tend to use hamburger. However, we encourage you to try ground turkey for a change of taste. It is an economical way to cut down your consumption of red meat and the calories and fat content are lower than regular ground chuck.

In addition, the fat in poultry is less saturated than that of meat and it is believed that the amount of saturation of the fat is critical to the development of cholesterol in the body. The American Heart Association recommends ingesting less saturated fat as well as less fat in general.

Here's a complete and tasty meal in 10 minutes!

NOT SO ORIGINAL JOE'S SPECIAL

> ¾ pound lean ground turkey
> ½ cup chopped onion
> 1 clove minced garlic
> 1 cup sliced mushrooms (¼ pound)
> 1 teaspoon salt
> ¼ teaspoon dried oregano
> 2 cups chopped fresh spinach
> 2 eggs + 1 egg white

Brown turkey, onion and garlic in non-stick frying pan. Add mushrooms, salt, oregano and spinach. Cook over medium heat until mushrooms and spinach are cooked (about 5 minutes).

Beat eggs well, add to mixture, cook and stir just until eggs are set. Serves 4. PER SERVING: 240 CALORIES, 11.5 GRAMS FAT.

This is a "de-fatted" variation of a popular hamburger casserole, a version of which many of you have probably made. The original calls for 1 pound of beef, sour cream, cream cheese, cheddar cheese and cottage cheese. Our fat cells loved it! You'll find this to be equally creamy but not nearly so rich.

HEARTY MEAT CASSEROLE

1 pound lean ground turkey or beef
1 chopped onion
1 clove minced garlic
½ teaspoon dried basil
½ teaspoon dried oregano
½ teaspoon salt
1 cup tomato sauce
¾ cup lowfat cottage cheese
¼ cup lowfat yogurt
6 ounces noodles, cooked and drained
¾ cup shredded part-skim mozzarella cheese

Starting with a cold, non-stick frying pan, brown ground meat slowly, breaking into small chunks. Add onion and garlic and cook for 2 minutes. Stir in spices and tomato sauce and heat briefly until sauce is thick and bubbling.

Meanwhile, blend together cottage cheese and yogurt until smooth. In a 9" x 13" baking dish, spread half of the noodles in a thin layer. Top with half of the meat sauce and all of the cottage cheese mixture, then repeat the layers of noodles and meat. Top with mozzarella cheese.

Bake at 350 degrees for 45 minutes or until cheese is browned and casserole bubbles. Serves 8. PER SERVING WITH TURKEY: 190 CALORIES, 7.5 GRAMS FAT.

CABBAGE ROLLS

    1 large head cabbage
    ½ pound lean ground beef, lamb or turkey
    ½ cup finely chopped onion
    2 cups cooked brown rice
    ¼ teaspoon garlic powder
    ¼ teaspoon dried oregano
    ¼ teaspoon dried thyme
    1 teaspoon salt
    1 cup tomato sauce
    1 cup beef broth

Cut out core of cabbage and drop head into large pot of boiling water until leaves begin to separate. Remove from water and separate leaves while still warm; drain well and cool.

Meanwhile, starting with cold, non-stick pan, brown meat slowly, breaking it up into small bits. Add onion and cook 5 minutes. Pour off any accumulated juices and fat. Add rice, garlic, oregano, thyme and salt and mix thoroughly.

Place a small amount on each leaf, roll up and place seam side down in non-stick baking dish. Combine tomato sauce and broth and pour over rolls. Bake at 350 degrees for one hour. Serves 4. PER SERVING WITH LEAN BEEF: 220 CALORIES, 6 GRAMS FAT.

NOTE: This recipe freezes well so double the recipe and put some away for a rainy night - pop them directly into the oven from the freezer, bake at 350 degrees for 1½ hours.

STUFFED ZUCCHINI BOATS

1 pound lean ground turkey or beef
1 finely chopped onion
1 finely chopped green pepper
1 teaspoon salt
¼ teaspoon garlic powder
¼ teaspoon dried oregano
1 cup stewed tomatoes
1 cup tomato sauce
2 medium zucchini (about 1½ pounds)
2 tablespoons grated Parmesan cheese

Starting with a cold, non-stick pan, brown ground meat slowly, breaking into very small chunks. Add onion and green pepper, brown briefly. Add salt, garlic powder, oregano, tomatoes and tomato sauce and cook until thick (about 30 minutes).

Meanwhile, halve zucchini lengthwise and remove pulp with tip of spoon, leaving a ½ inch shell. Fill the shells with meat mixture.

Spray baking dish with cooking spray, put filled shells in dish, cover with foil and bake until bubbly. Sprinkle with grated cheese and heat briefly to melt cheese. Serves 4.   PER SERVING WITH TURKEY: 230 CALORIES, 10 GRAMS FAT.

No additional fat is needed in the frying pan when using ground meat. Just start with a cold, non-stick pan. To remove all surface fat from the meat, pour it into a strainer once it has browned, let it drain, then turn out onto a double layer of paper towels and blot dry. Use the slight amount of fat remaining in the pan to brown any vegetables.

LAMB PITAS

   1 pound lean ground lamb
   1 chopped onion
   1 clove minced garlic
   2 cups stewed tomatoes
1½ cups chicken broth
   ¼ teaspoon dried oregano
   1 teaspoon salt
   1 cup brown rice
   4 cups fresh chopped spinach or lettuce
   4 pita breads, cut in half to make pockets
   ¼ cup Mock Sour Cream, p. 170

Starting with cold, non-stick frying pan, heat lamb slowly until lightly browned on all sides. Add onion and garlic and cook until limp. Stir in tomatoes, broth, oregano and salt and bring to a boil. Add brown rice, cover and simmer for 45 minutes or until rice is tender. Stir spinach or lettuce into lamb/rice mixture just before serving and heat through.

Meanwhile, in warm oven, heat pita bread until warm. Remove from oven, spread inside with Mock Sour Cream and stuff. Fills 8 pita halves. PER SERVING (filling only): 200 CALORIES, 4 GRAMS FAT.

Another "quickie"!

STROGANOFF

   1 pound lean ground turkey or beef
   1 teaspoon oil
   2 cups sliced mushrooms (½ pound)
  ½ cup finely chopped onion
   1 clove minced garlic
   2 tablespoons flour
   1 cup chicken broth
  ½ cup white wine
   1 teaspoon salt
   1 cup lowfat yogurt

Starting with a cold, non-stick pan, brown ground meat slowly. Remove from pan, add oil, mushrooms, onions and garlic and cook briefly until mushrooms are browned.

Stir in flour until well blended, add chicken broth and wine. Bring to boil, stirring constantly until thickened and smooth. Return meat to pan to warm through, add salt and simmer for 5 minutes. Stir in yogurt. Serves 4. PER SERVING WITH TURKEY: 285 CALORIES, 11 GRAMS FAT.

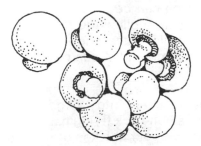

If using ground beef instead of turkey in this next recipe, omit the poultry seasoning and substitute ¼ teaspoon oregano.

TURKEY MEATLOAF

> 1 pound lean ground turkey
> ½ cup dry bread crumbs
> ¼ cup finely chopped onion
> 1 egg
> 1 tablespoon chicken broth (or water)
> 1 tablespoon Worcestershire sauce
> ½ teaspoon salt
> ½ teaspoon poultry seasoning
> ¼ cup chile sauce
> 2 tablespoons water

Combine all ingredients except chile sauce and water. Pat into a 4" x 8" loaf pan and bake at 325 degrees for 1 hour. Mix together chile sauce and water and baste frequently with this mixture. Serves 4. PER SERVING: 260 CALORIES, 12 GRAMS FAT.

SALISBURY STEAKS

The above recipe can be made into Salisbury Steaks for a quicker meal. Follow the recipe above EXCEPT instead of the chile sauce and water, mix together 1 teaspoon cornstarch and ½ cup chicken broth and set aside.

Shape the meat mixture into 4 large patties and brown them slowly in a non-stick frying pan. When cooked to desired doneness, pour chicken broth mixture into pan and stir until thick and smooth. Serves 4.

This is a good "make-ahead" casserole.

MEDITERRANEAN MACARONI

½ pound lean ground turkey, lamb or beef
¼ cup chopped onion
1 cup dry macaroni, cooked (4 ounces)
½ cup tomato sauce
½ teaspoon dried thyme
¼ teaspoon ground cinnamon
½ teaspoon salt
½ cup grated cheddar cheese

Starting with a cold non-stick frying pan, cook ground meat and onion until meat is browned; drain any fat. Stir in cooked macaroni, tomato sauce, thyme, cinnamon and salt.

Spread mixture into an 8" x 8" baking dish. Top with grated cheddar cheese. Bake in a 375 degree oven about 35 minutes. Serves 4. PER SERVING WITH TURKEY: 255 CALORIES, 10 GRAMS FAT.

NOTE: Don't overcook macaroni — keep it slightly "chewy" since it gets additional cooking in the casserole.

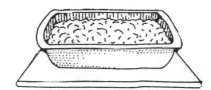

MEAL-SAVER MEAT SAUCE

    2 pounds lean ground meat
    2 chopped onions
    1 chopped green pepper
    2 cloves crushed garlic
    1 teaspoon salt, or to taste
    ½ teaspoon dried oregano
    ½ teaspoon dried basil
    4 cups tomato sauce
    1 tablespoon Worcestershire sauce
    ½ cup red wine

Starting with a cold, non-stick frying pan, brown the meat slowly, then remove from pan. Add onion and green pepper to pan and brown briefly.

Place meat and vegetables in heavy pot, add garlic, salt, oregano, basil, tomato sauce, Worcestershire sauce and wine. Bring to a boil, then simmer gently for 2 hours or until thick. Makes about 6 cups. PER HALF CUP SERVING WITH LEAN BEEF: 150 CALORIES, 3 GRAMS FAT.

This is the basic seasoning. From here, you can add chile powder, hot sauce and kidney beans for a quick bowl of CHILI; mix in some enchilada sauce and fill a TACO; add sliced mushrooms, more garlic and Worcestershire sauce for a SPAGHETTI sauce - use your imagination. One thing you don't add - a lot of extra effort when it comes to meal-making! A large batch made ahead and kept in the freezer will have endless uses.

LASAGNE

1 cup lowfat cottage cheese
1 cup part-skim ricotta cheese
3 cups Meal-Saver Meat Sauce
1 cup grated part-skim mozzarella cheese
½ cup grated Parmesan cheese
8 ounces dry lasagne noodles, cooked

Blend together cottage cheese and ricotta until smooth. In a 9" x 13" baking dish, arrange 1/3 of the noodles, 1/3 of the meat sauce, 1/3 of the ricotta-cottage cheese mixture and half of the mozzarella cheese.

Repeat layers of noodles, sauce, ricotta-cottage cheese and mozzarella. Top with remaining noodles, meat sauce, ricotta-cottage cheese and Parmesan cheese.

Bake at 350 degrees for 30 minutes or until very hot and bubbly. Serves 8. PER SERVING: 340 CALORIES, 9.5 GRAMS FAT.

NOTE: This casserole freezes nicely! For smaller families, divide it into two 8" square pans and bake one, freeze the other. To cook the frozen lasagne, preheat oven to 350 degrees and bake for approximately 1½ hours.

MID-WEEK MANICOTTI

NOODLES:

1 package manicotti noodles (12)
salted boiling water

Cook noodles according to package directions until JUST TENDER. Drain and place in pot of cold water until ready to stuff. (Best to have filling ready to go before cooking noodles.)

FILLING:

Thaw 2 cups Meal-Saver Sauce, (p. 106) and fill each manicotti noodle with about 3 tablespoons. Set aside while preparing sauce.

SAUCE AND CHEESE TOPPING:

2 cups tomato sauce
¼ teaspoon dried basil
¼ teaspoon dried oregano
⅛ teaspoon garlic powder
1 cup grated part-skim mozzarella cheese

Heat tomato sauce until bubbling and add basil, oregano and garlic. Spread a thin layer of sauce in a 9" x 13" baking dish. Place filled manicotti over sauce and spread remaining sauce on top. Cover with grated cheese.

All of the above can be done ahead of time. When ready to eat, bake the manicotti, uncovered, in a 350 degree oven for about 20 minutes or until sauce is hot and cheese is completely melted. Serves 4-5. Makes 12 filled manicotti. EACH: 160 CALORIES, 2.5 GRAMS FAT.

This version combines turkey and cheese for a milder taste with less emphasis on tomato.

MEAT 'N CHEESE MANICOTTI

FILLING:

¾ pound lean ground turkey
½ cup part-skim ricotta cheese
½ cup lowfat cottage cheese
½ teaspoon salt
⅛ teaspoon garlic powder

Spread turkey chunks on a broiler pan and broil until cooked, then chop in food processor until finely minced. Place in a mixing bowl, along with cheeses, salt and garlic powder. Mixture should be smooth.

Cook noodles and prepare sauce and cheese topping as indicated on previous page.

Fill each noodle with about 3 tablespoons of filling. Place filled manicotti over thin layer of sauce in baking dish and spread remaining sauce over top. Cover with grated cheese.

Bake at 350 degrees for 20 minutes or until sauce is bubbly. Makes 12. EACH: 170 CALORIES, 5 GRAMS FAT.

HOT POT

1 pound lean ground turkey
¼ teaspoon ground ginger
1 tablespoon cornstarch
1 tablespoon dry sherry
½ teaspoon salt
1 egg
2 carrots, sliced ⅛ inch thick
8 green onions, sliced diagonally
¼ pound sliced mushrooms
½ head shredded green cabbage
4 cups chicken broth
2 teaspoons soy sauce
2 ounces thin noodles

Mix turkey, ginger, cornstarch, sherry, salt and egg together. Shape into 1 inch balls; set aside. Heat broth and soy sauce to boiling in a 4 quart pan.

Add turkey balls and simmer 5 minutes.

One at a time, add carrots, onions, mushrooms, cabbage and noodles; let broth return to a simmer after each addition, about 6 minutes total. Serve into individual bowls. Serves 4. PER SERVING: 300 CALORIES, 12 GRAMS FAT.

That's Some Meatball

A light 'n spicy Middle-Eastern flavor

PICADILLO PEPPERS

>   2 large green peppers, parboiled*
>   ½ pound lean ground turkey or lamb
>   1 cup chopped onion
>   1 clove minced garlic
>   1 cup tomato sauce
>   ½ cup raisins
>   2 teaspoons chili powder
>   ½ teaspoon cinnamon
>   ½ teaspoon salt
>   ⅛ teaspoon cloves
>   1 cup cooked brown rice
>   2 cups stewed tomatoes

*Parboil the peppers by plunging them into boiling water for 10 minutes or until nearly tender, then plunge them immediately into cold water to stop the cooking process.

Starting with a cold, non-stick frying pan, brown ground meat slowly, breaking into very small chunks. Remove meat from pan, add onion and garlic and cook for 2 minutes.

Stir in tomato sauce, raisins and spices. Simmer mixture for 15 minutes. Stir in brown rice, mix well and fill parboiled peppers which have been cut in half.

Place peppers in baking dish and pour over and around them the tomatoes (Italian plum tomatoes best). Bake at 350 degrees for 15 minutes. Serves 4. PER SERVING WITH TURKEY: 240 CALORIES, 6 GRAMS FAT. (WITH LAMB, 260 CALORIES, 4 GRAMS FAT.)

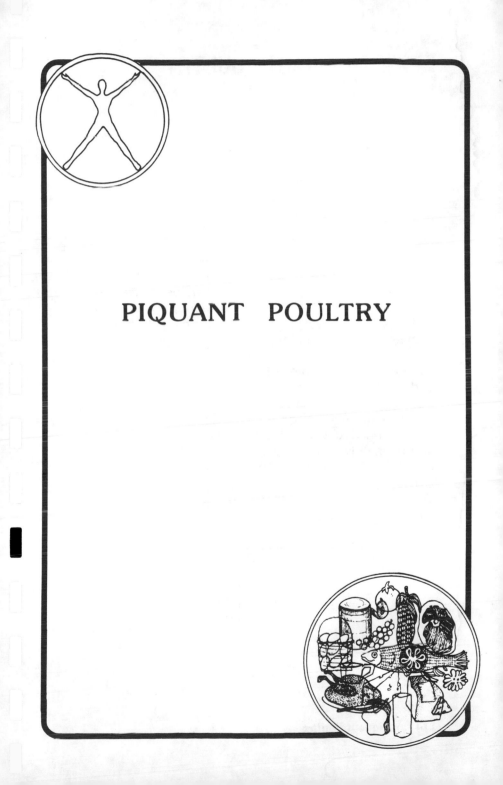

PIQUANT POULTRY

PIQUANT POULTRY

You have a choice of using either chicken thighs or chicken breasts in most of these recipes. We have suggested this in the interests of economy and practicality since the least expensive cut-up chicken comes with both breasts and thighs!

Obviously chicken pieces vary in size so the calories and fat grams have to be approximate. Whenever a choice is given, the calculations are based on the use of thighs. However, using skinned chicken breasts instead of skinned thighs will cut the calories and fat grams approximately in half. MOST RECIPES WILL HAVE LESS THAN 5 GRAMS OF FAT IF WHITE MEAT IS USED. Fat content is not high in either case but if you are being extra careful with your fat consumption, pay more and consume less!

COQ AU VIN

8 chicken thighs or 4 breasts, skinned
1 teaspoon oil
1 clove minced garlic
1 cup sliced mushrooms
½ teaspoon salt
¼ teaspoon dried thyme
1 bay leaf
1 cup red wine
1 cup chicken broth
1 teaspoon oil
20 small pearl onions
¼ cup chicken broth
2 teaspoons cornstarch
2 teaspoons water

Brown chicken well in oil and remove from pan. Add garlic and mushrooms and cook briefly; remove from pan. Return the chicken to the pan and add herbs, wine and 1 cup broth. Bring to a boil, then cover and simmer 30 minutes.

Meanwhile, in a separate pan, brown the onions in the second teaspoon of oil, add ¼ cup chicken broth and simmer 30 minutes. They should be tender but still have a firm shape.

At the end of the 30 minutes of chicken cooking, add reserved mushrooms and braised onions to chicken and cook an additional 10 minutes. Lift out chicken and vegetables to a serving dish and keep warm. Boil cooking liquid until reduced by half, mix cornstarch and water to a smooth paste and add to remaining juices, boil 1-2 minutes until thickened. Pour over chicken and vegetables. Serves 4. PER SERVING: 350 CALORIES, 11 GRAMS FAT.

CHICKEN MARENGO

  8 chicken thighs or 4 half breasts, skinned
  1 teaspoon oil
  ½ cup white wine
  ½ cup chicken broth
  2 cups stewed tomatoes
  1 bay leaf
  ¼ teaspoon dried thyme
  1 teaspoon oil
20 small pearl onions
  1 cup mushrooms, cut in ¼'s
  1 minced garlic clove

Brown chicken in first teaspoon oil; add wine, broth, tomatoes, bay leaf and thyme. Cover and simmer 15 minutes.

Meanwhile, in separate pan, heat second teaspoon oil and brown onions, mushrooms and garlic. Add to chicken mixture and simmer an additional 30 minutes. Serves 4. PER SERVING: 300 CALORIES, 9 GRAMS FAT.

SHAKE A LEG!

12 chicken legs, skinned
 ¼ cup Shake 'n Bake

Moisten chicken legs with water, roll in Shake 'n Bake to coat thoroughly. Place on non-stick baking sheet (no added fat) and bake at 400 degrees for approximately 45 minutes, until coating is brown and crusty. EACH: 50-60 CALORIES, 1.5-2 GRAMS FAT, depending on size of legs.

Quick yet elegant.

CHICKEN CHABLIS

4 half chicken breasts, skinned and boned
1 teaspoon oil
⅛ teaspoon garlic powder
⅛ teaspoon oregano
2 cups thinly sliced zucchini
¼ cup chicken broth
¼ cup lemon juice
¼ cup white wine
    salt and pepper to taste

Brown chicken in hot, non-stick pan. Sprinkle with garlic powder and oregano. In separate skillet, heat oil and lightly brown zucchini slices. Layer zucchini over chicken, add broth and lemon juice, cover and simmer 10 minutes or until chicken is done.

Remove chicken and zucchini to serving plates, add wine to juices in pan, boil briefly and pour over chicken. Serves 4. PER SERVING: 140 CALORIES, 3 GRAMS FAT.

CHINESE CHICKEN

½ cup chicken broth
¼ cup soy sauce
2 tablespoons dry sherry
1 tablespoon cornstarch
2 teaspoons oil
2 whole chicken breasts, skinned and boned
1 clove minced garlic
1 cup sliced mushrooms
2 cups snow peas
8 ounce can water chestnuts
6 ounce can bamboo shoots

Shake together broth, soy sauce, sherry and cornstarch until smooth. Set aside.

Cut chicken into 1 inch cubes. Heat oil in large pan or wok and brown chicken quickly. Remove from pan and keep warm.

Add garlic, mushrooms and snow peas; stir for 2 minutes until mushrooms are slightly browned.

Return chicken to pan, add water chestnuts and bamboo shoots, pour well-mixed sauce over all and cook for 2-3 minutes until chicken is done and vegetables are crisp-tender. Serves 4. PER SERVING: 200 CALORIES, 5 GRAMS FAT.

CHINESE CHICKEN II

2 whole chicken breasts, skinned and boned
3 tablespoons soy sauce
2 teaspoons oil
½ cup sliced celery
¼ cup chopped green onion
2 cups broccoli florets
½ cup chicken broth
¼ teaspoon garlic powder
8 ounce can water chestnuts
6 ounce can bamboo shoots
2 tablespoons soy sauce
1 tablespoon lemon juice
½ cup chicken broth
1 tablespoon cornstarch

Cut chicken into 1 inch cubes and marinate in soy sauce for one hour. Heat oil in large skillet or wok, remove chicken from marinade and brown quickly in oil until white and firm (about 2 minutes). Remove and keep warm.

Brown celery and onions Add broccoli, ½ cup chicken broth and garlic powder. Cover and cook until broccoli is tender (about 5 minutes - do not overcook).

Return chicken to vegetables, cook all together for 3 minutes. Add water chestnuts and bamboo shoots. Stir briefly to heat.

Mix together soy sauce, lemon juice, chicken broth and cornstarch and pour over all; heat well. Serves 4. PER SERVING: 180 CALORIES, 5 GRAMS FAT.

EASY EVERYDAY ROAST CHICKEN

        1 roasting chicken
          salt
        ¼ teaspoon poultry seasoning
        ½ lemon
        ½ cup thinly sliced onion
        ½ cup chicken broth

Place chicken breast-side down in heavy Dutch oven sprayed with cooking spray. Sprinkle with salt and poultry seasoning and squeeze the juice of half a lemon over all. Roast uncovered for ½ hour, then turn chicken breast-side up and layer onions over top. Baste with chicken broth and continue roasting for an additional ½ hour or until thermometer reads 185 degrees. Pour off pan juices, separate from fat and serve as a gravy.

Easy, inexpensive and colorful.

CONFETTI CHICKEN

        1 cup diced carrot
        1 cup diced celery
        ½ cup diced onion
        ¼ teaspoon dried thyme
        ¼ teaspoon dried oregano
        ½ teaspoon salt
        8 chicken thighs, skinned
        ½ cup white wine
        ½ cup water
        ¼ cup lemon juice

Mix diced vegetables, herbs and salt together and layer in an 8" x 8" baking dish. Brown chicken thighs in non-stick pan and place on bed of vegetables.

Mix together wine, water and lemon juice and pour over chicken. Cover and bake at 325 degrees for 45 minutes. Serves 4. PER SERVING: 265 CALORIES, 8 GRAMS FAT.

Spicy and hot, but with cool undertones!

CURRIED CHICKEN

8 chicken thighs, skin removed
1 cup lowfat yogurt
1 teaspoon curry powder
½ teaspoon ground cumin
1 teaspoon salt
½ teaspoon garlic powder
¼ teaspoon cayenne pepper
1 teaspoon oil
1 chopped onion
2 cups chopped tomatoes
1 teaspoon cornstarch
1 teaspoon water

Mix together yogurt and spices. Coat chicken with mixture and let stand at room temperature for 1 hour (or refrigerate for up to 4 hours).

Heat oil in a non-stick skillet, add onion and brown lightly. Stir in tomatoes and add chicken plus marinade. Mix well, cover and simmer for about 30 minutes.

If desired, thicken juices with 1 teaspoon cornstarch mixed with 1 teaspoon water. Serves 4. PER SERVING: 300 CALORIES, 10 GRAMS FAT.

The following recipe does have some fat in it - a small amount to flavor the mushrooms and 1 tablespoon of cream per person to give it the final "French touch"! But it's worth it for a special occasion - and take a look at the following recipe to see what it could have been - it has been included just to help you see how your own favorite recipes can be "de-fatted"!

COMPANY BEST CHICKEN SUPREME

    4 half chicken breasts, boned and skinned
    2 teaspoons margarine
    1 cup sliced mushrooms (¼ pound)
    1 clove crushed garlic
    ½ cup dry white wine
    ½ teaspoon salt
    ½ cup chicken broth
    1 teaspoon cornstarch
    ¼ cup light cream
    2 teaspoons lemon juice

Brown chicken breasts slowly on both sides in 1 teaspoon of the margarine. Remove from pan, add second teaspoon of margarine, mushrooms and garlic and stir until lightly browned.

Return chicken to pan, add wine and salt. Simmer for about 10 minutes, until chicken breasts are done (when pierced with fork, juices should not be pink).

Shake together chicken broth and cornstarch, add to pan juices and mix well. Boil 1-2 minutes until thick, stir in cream and heat briefly until sauce is thickened slightly. Add lemon juice to taste. Serves 4. PER SERVING: 230 CALORIES, 12 GRAMS FAT.

DANGER:

THE FOLLOWING RECIPE IS FOR COMPARISON ONLY!!

THE ORIGINAL SUPREMES

4 half chicken breasts, boned and skinned
5 tablespoons butter
1 cup sliced mushrooms (¼ pound)
¼ cup chicken broth
¼ cup dry vermouth
1 cup heavy cream

Brown the chicken and mushrooms in butter. Cover and cook until done, about 10 minutes.

Pour the broth into the casserole with the cooking butter and boil down quickly until syrupy. Stir in the cream and boil down until cream has thickened slightly. Serves 4. PER SERVING: 500 CALORIES, 40 GRAMS FAT.

NOTE: It is not unusual to see recipes with 40 to 50 grams of fat per serving - watch out for them and try to figure out what you can do to lower the fat content!

SPRING CHICKEN

2 whole chicken breasts, skinned and boned
2 tablespoons soy sauce
1 tablespoon dry sherry
1 tablespoon water
1 tablespoon cornstarch
1 teaspoon oil
1 cup sliced celery
1 cup sliced asparagus
¼ cup sliced green onion
1 cup small button mushrooms

Cut chicken into 1 inch cubes. Mix together soy sauce, sherry, water and cornstarch and shake well. Pour over the chicken and marinate for one hour.

Slice vegetables on the diagonal. Heat oil in large non-stick frying pan or wok. Remove chicken from marinade, reserving juices, and brown in hot oil. Remove from pan and keep warm. Add vegetables to pan and cook for 5 minutes. Return chicken to pan and heat briefly until mixture is hot. Pour in the reserved marinade and boil quickly until thick. Serves 2. PER SERVING: 280 CALORIES, 4 GRAMS FATS.

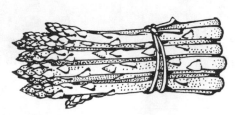

CHICKEN CORDON BLEU

4 half chicken breasts, skinned and boned
4 thin slices turkey ham (2 ounces)
4 thin slices mozzarella cheese (1 ounce)
1 teaspoon oil
¼ teaspoon dried thyme
⅔ cup chicken broth
¼ cup white wine
¼ cup lemon juice
    salt and pepper to taste

Pound chicken breasts until approximately ¼ inch thick. On top of each flat breast place a slice of turkey ham and a slice of cheese. Roll up chicken, tucking in ends, and secure with toothpicks. (This can be done ahead of time; refrigerate rolls until ready to cook.)

Heat oil in non-stick pan and brown chicken rolls on all sides. Sprinkle with thyme and pour broth over rolls. Cover tightly and simmer 15 minutes. Remove chicken breasts and keep warm.

Increase heat, add wine and lemon juice to pan juices and boil down sauce until reduced by half. Add salt and pepper to taste. Serves 4 elegantly! PER SERVING: 170 CALORIES, 5 GRAMS FAT.

This is an elegant company dinner - it looks more complicated than it is and can all be done ahead of time.

CHICKEN CANNELLONI

CREPES:

3 eggs
1 cup skim milk
⅔ cup flour

Beat eggs and milk together, add flour and beat well until completely mixed. Let stand about 30 minutes and beat again before cooking. To make crepes, heat 7 inch non-stick skillet or crepe pan until medium hot, quickly pour in 2 tablespoons batter for each crepe and tilt pan to cover bottom evenly. Cook until underside is lightly browned, about 1 minute, then turn over and brown other side about 20 seconds. Remove and cool before filling. Makes 16 crepes.

FILLING:

1 teaspoon oil
¼ cup minced onion
¼ cup sliced mushrooms
½ cup cooked spinach, drained well
1 whole chicken breast, poached, no skin
½ cup part-skim ricotta cheese
½ cup lowfat cottage cheese
½ teaspoon salt
2 teaspoons lemon juice

Heat oil, cook onion and mushrooms briefly. Mince cooked chicken and add to vegetables along with all other ingredients. The result will be a fairly solid mixture. Place about 2 tablespoons in the center of each crepe and roll crepe around filling, tucking the ends under to form a small packet. Set aside.

SAUCE AND CHEESE TOPPING:

1 cup skim milk
½ teaspoon salt
1 tablespoon cornstarch
3 cups tomato sauce
1 cup chicken broth
¼ teaspoon dried basil
¼ teaspoon dried oregano
⅛ teaspoon garlic powder
¼ teaspoon onion powder
1 cup shredded part-skim mozzarella cheese

Blend a small amount of the skim milk with salt and cornstarch; when smooth, add this mixture to remaining milk and bring to a boil in small saucepan. Boil until thick, then set aside.

Meanwhile, mix together tomato sauce, chicken broth and herbs. Simmer this mixture about 45 minutes or until it is reduced to 2 cups.

Stir together the thickened milk sauce and the tomato sauce.

Spread a thin layer of sauce on the bottom of a 9" x 13" baking dish and place filled crepes on sauce. Spread remaining sauce over crepes and top with grated cheese.

Bake at 350 degrees for 20 minutes or until sauce is bubbly. Makes 16 crepes, serves 4-6. EACH CREPE: 115 CALORIES, 4 GRAMS FAT.

CHICKEN CACCIATORE

1 teaspoon oil
8 chicken thighs or 4 half breasts, skinned
1 chopped onion
1 clove minced garlic
1 teaspoon salt
1 bay leaf
¼ teaspoon dried oregano
¼ teaspoon dried basil
½ cup white wine
1 cup stewed tomatoes
1 cup tomato sauce
1 cup sliced mushrooms

Heat oil in a non-stick skillet and brown chicken, onion and garlic. Add all other ingredients except mushrooms. Bring to a boil, then cover and simmer about 30 minutes. Add mushrooms, cook 10 minutes more.

Remove chicken from pan, boil down sauce until slightly thickened. Serves 4. PER SERVING: 300 CALORIES, 9 GRAMS FAT.

Put this together ahead of time and pop it into the oven when you come home!

'FOILED' CHICKEN

chicken breasts, skinned half per person
salt, garlic powder, onion powder
dried dill, lemon juice

For each packet: place one chicken breast in center of a 12-inch foil square. Sprinkle with herbs. Squeeze ½ lemon over each breast, bring up edges and seal.

Bake at 350 degrees 30 minutes or until juices are no longer pink. Remove from oven, turn on broiler. Roll chicken in accumulated juices, place under broiler 2-3 minutes or until browned. PER SERVING: 120 CALORIES, 2 GRAMS FAT.

FRENCH COUNTRY CHICKEN

8 chicken thighs, skinned
4 sliced onions
1 tablespoon Dijon mustard
1½ cups dry white wine
1 bay leaf
¼ teaspoon dried thyme
½ teaspoon salt

Spray a non-stick skillet with cooking spray. Add chicken to pan and heat slowly until lightly browned on both sides. Layer sliced onions over chicken.

Mix together mustard, wine and spices and pour over chicken and onions. Cover and simmer for ½ hour. Uncover pan and continue cooking until most of the liquid has evaporated. If desired, brown chicken under broiler just before serving. Serves 4. PER SERVING: 350 CALORIES, 9 GRAMS FAT.

CHICKEN CHOP SUEY

2 teaspoons oil, divided
1 whole chicken breast, skinned and boned
2 cups chopped cabbage
1 cup chopped green pepper
1 cup chopped onion
2 cups diagonally sliced fresh asparagus
1 cup bean sprouts
1 tablespoon soy sauce
1 tablespoon dry sherry
½ cup chicken broth
1 tablespoon cornstarch

Heat 1 teaspoon oil in large, non-stick skillet or wok.
Cut chicken into 1 inch cubes and brown quickly.
Remove from pan and keep warm.

Heat second teaspoon oil in same pan and add all vegetables except bean sprouts. Stir-fry over high heat until
crisp-tender. Return chicken to pan, add bean sprouts,
cover and cook 3 minutes.

Mix together soy sauce, sherry, broth and cornstarch
and pour over vegetables and chicken. Bring to a boil
and cook 1 minute or until thick. Serves 4. PER
SERVING: 150 CALORIES, 3.5 GRAMS FAT.

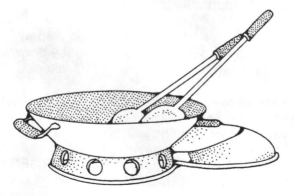

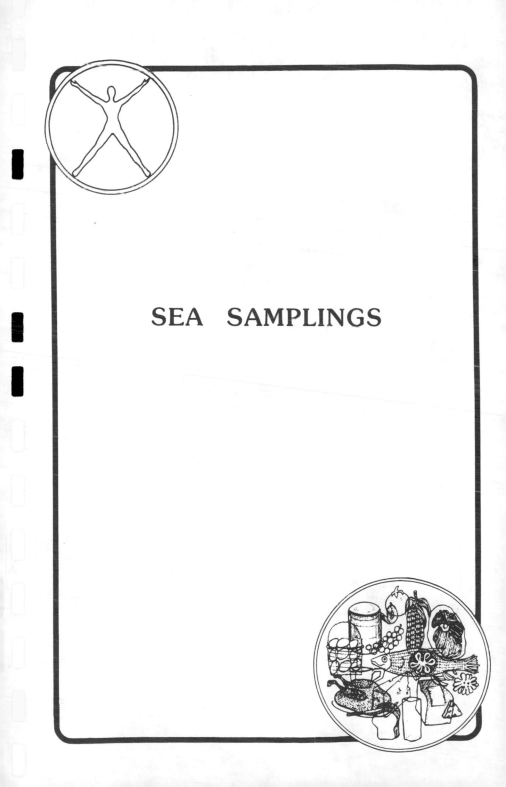

SEA SAMPLINGS

SEA SAMPLINGS

BAKED RED SNAPPER

1½ pounds thick red snapper fillets
½ lemon, juice and grated rind
⅛ teaspoon thyme
1 clove minced garlic
½ cup chopped celery
½ cup chopped green pepper
¼ cup chopped onion
1 teaspoon oil
1 cup diced fresh tomatoes
1 teaspoon cornstarch
1 teaspoon water

Place fish in baking dish. Mix lemon, thyme and garlic together and spread over fish. Let fish stand in refrigerator 1 hour.

Meanwhile, brown celery, green pepper and onion in oil. Add tomatoes and spread vegetable mixture over fish.

Bake at 375 degrees for 10 to 20 minutes or until fish flakes. Remove from oven, pour off liquid into sauce pan and keep fish warm.

Thicken sauce by adding cornstarch/water mixture and boiling gently. Pour sauce over fish. Serves 4. PER SERVING: 180 CALORIES, 3 GRAMS FAT.

NOTE: The general rule for fish is to cook it approximately 10 minutes per inch of thickness. Do not use thin fillets in this recipe — they would completely fall apart during baking.

A real Country French dinner - enjoy it with fresh asparagus for color contrast and brown rice to soak up the juices.

COQUILLES

¼ cup minced onion
1 cup sliced mushrooms
2 tablespoons finely chopped green onion
1 clove minced garlic
1 teaspoon oil
1 pound scallops
   flour
½ cup dry vermouth
¼ cup water
⅛ teaspoon dried dill
   salt and pepper to taste
2 teaspoons lemon juice
¼ cup heavy cream
¼ cup grated part-skim mozzarella cheese

Cook onions, mushrooms and garlic in 1 teaspoon oil for 5 minutes. Cut scallops into ½ inch pieces, dip them in flour and add to pan to brown lightly. Add vermouth, water and dill and simmer 5 minutes.

Remove vegetables and scallops from sauce and divide into four individual serving dishes. Boil sauce until thick, add salt, pepper, lemon juice and cream. Pour sauce equally over each serving. Top with grated cheese (1 tablespoon each). This much can be done ahead of time.

When ready to eat, heat the portions in a 350 degree oven for 15 minutes, then broil briefly until cheese is melted. Serves 4. PER SERVING: 185 CALORIES, 8 GRAMS FAT.

QUICK DEVILLED FISH

    1½ pounds sole fillets
    1 tablespoon horseradish
    1 tablespoon Dijon mustard
    1 tablespoon lemon juice
    1 tablespoon grated Parmesan cheese
    ¼ cup lowfat yogurt

Place fish in single layer in broiling pan sprayed with cooking spray. Mix the rest of the ingredients together and spread over fish. Broil 4 minutes, without turning. Serves 4. PER SERVING: 115 CALORIES, 1 GRAM FAT.

FISH FLORENTINE

    1 10 ounce package frozen cut spinach
    1 egg + 1 egg white, beaten together
    1½ cups cooked rice
    ¼ cup grated Parmesan cheese
    1 pound frozen fish fillets, partly thawed
    1 tablespoon lemon juice
    ⅛ teaspoon garlic powder

Cook spinach and combine with eggs, rice and Parmesan cheese. Place half of fish in bottom of loaf pan, spread spinach mixture on top, then cover with remaining fish.

Sprinkle garlic powder on fish, pour lemon juice over top, cover and bake at 350 degrees for about 40 minutes. Fish should flake and filling should be firm. Serves 4. PER SERVING: 220 CALORIES, 4 GRAMS FAT.

STUFFED SOLE

½ pound sliced mushrooms
1 teaspoon oil
½ pound shredded fresh spinach
¼ teaspoon garlic powder
¼ teaspoon dried oregano
1½ pounds sole fillets, in 4 pieces
4 teaspoons lemon juice
2 tablespoons grated mozzarella cheese
   paprika

Brown the mushrooms in oil until limp. Add spinach and cook for one minute. Remove from heat and drain. Add garlic powder and oregano.

Place one quarter of the mixture in the center of each fillet; roll and place in a baking dish sprayed with cooking spray. Sprinkle with lemon juice and top with cheese.

Bake 20 minutes in a 425 degree oven. Sprinkle a dash of paprika on each roll after removing from oven. Serves 4. PER SERVING: 150 CALORIES, 2 GRAMS FAT.

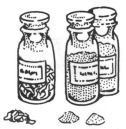

SHRIMPS IN A POT

1½ pounds medium shrimp or prawns
1 teaspoon oil
1 large chopped onion
1 28 ounce can plum tomatoes
½ cup dry white wine
1 tablespoon chopped fresh parsley
1 teaspoon dried oregano
   salt and pepper to taste
4 ounces crumbled feta cheese

Shell and devein shrimp, leaving tails attached. Heat oil and cook onion until tender, about 5 minutes. Add tomatoes (crush slightly), wine, half the parsley, oregano, salt and pepper. Bring to a boil, reduce heat, add shrimp and simmer about 3 minutes.

Turn mixture into an oven-proof casserole and crumble cheese over the top. Bake at 375 degrees for 15 minutes, just until cheese melts slightly. Sprinkle with remaining parsley. Serves 4. PER SERVING: 230 CALORIES, 3 GRAMS FAT.

NOTE: This can be prepared ahead to the point of putting the mixture into the casserole. Do not add the cheese until ready to bake.

FISHERMAN'S SHELLFISH STEW

24 clams in shell
1 pound medium raw prawns
1 pound compact white fish, e.g. halibut
1 large chopped onion
1 chopped green pepper
3 large chopped tomatoes
garlic powder
salt
1 cup dry white wine
1 cup tomato sauce

Scrub clams well, soak in water for 1 hour. Devein and shell prawns. Cut white fish into 2 inch cubes.

Drain and place clams in bottom of a heavy 4 quart Dutch oven. Over the clams make a layer consisting of 1/3 of the onions, 1/3 of the green pepper and 1/3 of the tomatoes Sprinkle with garlic powder and salt. Over this vegetable layer place half the prawns and half the white fish.

Repeat the vegetable layer, sprinkling with garlic powder and salt again, top with prawns and fish, and end with the third layer of vegetables.

Mix wine and tomato sauce together and pour over all ingredients. Bring to a boil, then cover and simmer for about 25 minutes or until clams open. Serves 4. PER SERVING: 350 CALORIES, 4 GRAMS FAT.

CIOPPINO

  1 chopped onion
  1 clove minced garlic
  1 teaspoon oil
  2 cups stewed tomatoes
  1 cup tomato sauce
  1 cup red wine
  1 cup water
  2 tablespoons wine vinegar
  ½ teaspoon dried basil
  ½ teaspoon dried oregano
  1 teaspoon salt
24 clams in shell
  1 pound halibut
  1 pound medium raw prawns
  1 whole crab, cleaned and cracked

Brown onion and garlic in oil, add all other ingredients except seafood and fish, bring to a boil, cover and simmer for 1 hour.

Meanwhile, scrub clams well, soak in cold water for 1 hour. Cut halibut into 2 inch cubes. Devein prawns by cutting a slit in the back of the shell and stripping out the black material. (Leave shell on.)

Drain clams and place in bottom of a heavy 4 quart Dutch oven. Over the clams layer the halibut, prawns and crab. Pour hot tomato sauce over all, cover and simmer about 25 minutes or until clam shells are open. Serves 6. PER SERVING: 250 CALORIES, 4 GRAMS FAT.

*Serve this stew with crusty French bread for "dunking".
This is a family favorite - costs little and is easily and
quickly prepared. You can use any bottom fish and we
guarantee you'll scrape the bottom to finish it off!*

"BOTTOMS-UP" CHOWDER

1 chopped onion
1 chopped green pepper
1 clove minced garlic
1 teaspoon oil
4 cups stewed tomatoes
½ teaspoon dried thyme
1 teaspoon salt
2 cups dry white wine
2 cups water
2 tablespoons lemon juice
2 potatoes, peeled and diced
2 pounds bottom fish, e.g. red snapper

Brown onion, green pepper and garlic in oil. Add
tomatoes, thyme, salt, wine, water and lemon juice.
Bring to a boil, simmer 30 minutes.

Add potatoes, cook 15 minutes. Cut fish in 1 inch
cubes, add to sauce and cook 2-3 minutes or just until
fish flakes. Serves 6. PER SERVING: 230 CALORIES,
2 GRAMS FAT.

CAUTION: Easy to overcook fish - be ready to eat
before you add it to the pot.

This recipe takes some advance planning but is very easily done in stages...and it can all be done ahead of time, ready for a final few minutes of cooking when guests have arrived. Serve with green salad, French bread and a bottle of chilled white wine for a light gourmet dinner.

SHRIMP AND SCALLOP CREPES

CREPES:

    2 eggs
    ⅔ cup skim milk
    ½ cup flour

Beat eggs and milk together, add flour and beat well until completely mixed. Let stand about 30 minutes and beat again before cooking.

Heat a 7 inch non-stick skillet or crepe pan until medium hot, quickly pour in 2 tablespoons batter for each crepe and swirl batter to cover bottom evenly. Cook until underside is lightly browned, about 1 minute, then turn over and brown other side about 20 seconds. Remove and cool before filling. Makes 12.

FILLING:

½ cup chicken broth
½ cup skim milk
¼ cup white wine
4 teaspoons cornstarch
¼ teaspoon dried dill
½ teaspoon salt
1 tablespoon lemon juice
½ cup shredded mozzarella cheese (divided)
¼ pound scallops, cut in ½ inch pieces
½ cup sliced mushrooms
¼ teaspoon dried dill
1 teaspoon lemon juice
¼ pound cooked tiny shrimp

In a 2 quart saucepan blend together broth, milk and wine. Mix a small amount of blended mixture with cornstarch until smooth then stir this into the rest of the liquid. Boil 1 minute or until smooth and thick. Add dill, salt, lemon juice and ¼ cup cheese. Measure out ½ cup sauce and set aside.

Poach scallops and mushrooms for 3 minutes in simmering water seasoned with dill and lemon juice. Drain and add scallops and mushrooms to the larger portion of sauce, along with shrimp.

Fill crepes, dividing seafood mixture equally. Roll up crepes and place in a 9" x 13" baking dish sprayed with cooking spray. Pour reserved sauce over crepes and top with remaining ¼ cup cheese. This can all be done ahead of time.

When ready to eat, heat the crepes for 15 minutes in a 350 degree oven, then broil briefly to brown the cheese. Serves 4. PER SERVING: 200 CALORIES, 6 GRAMS FAT.

If the sauce is prepared ahead of time, meal preparation will be a matter of minutes.

SCARLET SNAPPER

1 cup chopped onion
½ cup chopped green pepper
½ cup chopped celery
½ cup tomato sauce
½ cup white wine
¼ teaspoon garlic powder
½ teaspoon salt
1½ pounds red snapper fillets
½ lemon

Mix together all ingredients except snapper and lemon and simmer 30 minutes or until vegetables are tender and sauce is thick. (If done ahead, refrigerate until ready to cook fish.)

Broil snapper about 3 minutes per side and arrange on a warm serving dish. Squeeze half a lemon over the fish and pour a ribbon of sauce on top of each piece of fish. Serve the remaining sauce in a bowl. Serves 4.
PER SERVING: 140 CALORIES, 2 GRAMS FAT.

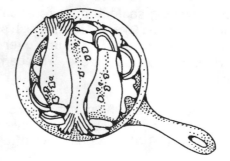

LIGHT 'N LIVELY

LIGHT 'N LIVELY

This is an unusual and juicy "knife and fork" sandwich.

TUNA ALASKA

> 1 7 ounce can water-packed tuna
> 2 tablespoons lowfat yogurt
> 1 tablespoon lowfat mayonnaise
> ¼ teaspoon dried dill
> 2 tablespoons lemon juice
> 1 tablespoon minced green onion
> salt and pepper to taste
> 1 egg white
> 1 tablespoon lowfat yogurt
> 2 slices whole wheat bread

Preheat broiler. Make a tuna salad with all ingredients except egg white and final tablespoon of yogurt. Toast 2 slices of bread. Spread tuna on toast and cover with beaten egg white. Be sure to spread it to the edges of the toast, covering the filling completely. Broil the sandwich until the meringue is cooked and brown. Serves 2. PER SERVING, filling only: 110 CALORIES, 2.5 GRAMS FAT.

LOWFAT, LOW CAL, HIGH FIBER AND FILLING — and easy and quick!! How can you do better?

'SIMPLE SAM'-WICH

Spread one slice of whole grain bread with Mustard-Mayo cream, p. 170. Pile on 1 — 2 ounces of thinly sliced turkey ham. Try it!

A delicious way to get some fiber!

CRUNCHY SHRIMP SALAD SANDWICH

- 6 ounces small shrimp
- 1 chopped celery stalk
- 1 chopped green onion
- 2 tablespoons Mock Sour Cream, p. 170
- 1 tablespoon lowfat mayonnaise
- 1 teaspoon lemon juice
- ⅛ teaspoon dried dill
  salt and pepper to taste
- 4 slices whole grain bread
  Mock Sour Cream
  sliced cucumbers
  alfalfa sprouts

Mix shrimp, celery, onion, Mock Sour Cream, mayonnaise, lemon juice, dill, salt and pepper. If you have a food processor put everything in it and give it two or three SHORT bursts (too much and you'll have a paste).

Spread whole grain bread with Mock Sour Cream. Layer thinly sliced cucumbers on two slices of bread, then shrimp mixture; top with alfalfa sprouts and remaining bread. Serves 2. PER SERVING, filling only: 100 CALORIES, 4 GRAMS FAT.

FRENCH DIP SANDWICH

½ cup beef broth
½ cup water
1 cup red wine
1 tablespoon Worcestershire sauce
1 pound flank steak
  garlic powder
  onion powder
  salt and pepper to taste
4 long crusty French rolls
  Mustard-Mayo Cream, p. 170

Heat together broth, water, wine and Worcestershire sauce to make the dipping broth. Season the steak with garlic powder, onion powder, salt and pepper to taste and broil until rare.

Toast French rolls by splitting them lengthwise and placing them cut side down in a hot, non-stick frying pan.

Meanwhile, spread one half of each roll with Mustard-Mayo Cream. Thinly slice the steak, saving the juices. Pour some juice over the bare half of each roll, pile on the meat, cover with the second half of the roll and serve along with a small cup of dipping broth. Serves 4. PER SERVING: 300 CALORIES, 7 GRAMS FAT.

SUNDAY SPECIAL OMELET

OMELET

2 eggs + 1 egg white
2 teaspoons lowfat yogurt
⅛ teaspoon dried dill
¼ teaspoon salt

FILLING:

½ teaspoon oil
2 tablespoons finely chopped onion
½ cup thinly sliced mushrooms
2 ounces diced turkey ham (about ½ cup)
½ cup chopped fresh tomatoes
1 teaspoon cornstarch
¼ cup chicken broth
2 tablespoons grated mozzarella cheese

Beat together eggs, egg white, yogurt, dill and salt. Set aside. In non-stick pan, heat oil and cook onion, mushrooms and turkey ham until vegetables are soft. Add tomatoes and simmer until mixture is thick. Mix together cornstarch and broth and stir into vegetable-ham mixture; bring to a boil then reduce heat and simmer until thick.

Meanwhile, heat a non-stick skillet and pour in eggs. Cook until almost set. Spoon filling over one half of the omelet and top with grated cheese. Fold the other half carefully over the filling. Cut into two portions and serve. Serves 2. PER SERVING: 180 CALORIES, 11.5 GRAMS FAT.

A frittata is a wonderful invention for busy nights and busy people. Basically, it is a mixture of vegetables, possibly some meat, eggs and a bit of cheese. Beyond that, almost anything goes. These examples show you "how" to do it — your own refrigerator will probably dictate exactly "what" you do.

FAST FRITTATA FOR TWO

    1 small zucchini or 4 asparagus spears*
    1 chopped green onion
    4 sliced mushrooms
    1 teaspoon oil
    2 ounces turkey ham
      salt and pepper
    2 eggs + 1 egg white
    ¼ cup grated part-skim mozzarella cheese
    2 tablespoons grated Parmesan cheese

*Slice zucchini or asparagus in thin, diagonal slices so they will cook quickly. Brown the vegetables in oil until crisp-tender. Add turkey ham, cut in ½ inch cubes or thin strips. Season mixture to taste.

Beat eggs and pour over vegetables, cover and cook until set. Preheat broiler, sprinkle on both cheeses and broil until melted. Serves 2. PER SERVING: 200 CALORIES, 9 GRAMS FAT.

To expand the stove-top frittata into a more substantial oven meal, try the following recipe.

OVEN FRITTATA FOR FOUR

1 teaspoon oil
1½ cups assorted raw vegetables
6 ounces diced turkey ham
½ cup skim milk
3 eggs + 2 egg whites
¼ cup grated part-skim mozzarella cheese
¼ cup rated sharp cheddar cheese

Heat oil, brown vegetables until crisp-tender. Add turkey ham. Beat milk and eggs together, stir in cheese and pour over vegetable-ham mixture. Pour into a 1 quart casserole dish sprayed with cooking spray and bake at 350 degrees for 20 minutes. Serves 4. PER SERVING: 175 CALORIES, 11 GRAMS FAT.

This is another "use up your leftovers" meal. It's great for lunch or a light supper. Again, you can use whatever vegetables you have on hand plus a small amount of protein. Try cooked broccoli or asparagus in place of the onions and mushrooms.

QUICK QUICHE

    1 cup cooked brown rice
    2 ounces turkey ham
    2 chopped green onions
    ¼ cup cooked mushrooms
    ½ cup grated sharp cheddar cheese
    3 eggs + 2 egg whites
 1½ cups skim milk
    ½ teaspoon salt

Spray 4 small custard dishes or tart pans (about 4 inch diameter) with cooking spray; press ¼ cup cooked rice into bottom of each pan. Sprinkle rice with turkey ham, green onion, mushrooms and cheese.

Beat together eggs, milk and salt and pour into pans. Bake at 350 degrees for about 20 minutes or until quiche is set. Serve hot or cold. Serves 4. PER SERVING: 210 CALORIES, 10 GRAMS FAT.

Instead of using 2 whole eggs, try adding 1 egg white to 1 whole egg whenever you want a reasonable serving of scrambled eggs or an omelet. A serving containing 2 yolks would have 500 milligrams of cholesterol or more, almost double the daily 300 milligrams permitted by the American Heart Association.

FRIED RICE

1 egg + 1 egg white, beaten together
2 teaspoons oil, divided
1 clove minced garlic
½ cup thinly sliced celery
¼ cup chopped green pepper
½ cup sliced green onion (reserve tops)
¼ cup thinly sliced carrot
2 cups cooked rice
1 cup bean sprouts
4 tablespoons soy sauce
1 tablespoon lemon juice
1 tablespoon dry sherry
¼ teaspoon ground ginger

Pour eggs into non-stick frying pan and cook just until set in one large pancake. Remove from pan, cool, cut into thin strips and reserve.

Heat 1 teaspoon oil in pan, then add garlic, celery, green pepper, green onion (not tops) and carrot. Brown, stirring constantly, for about 2 minutes.

Add second teaspoon of oil, then add cooked rice. Stir constantly until heated through and slightly browned. Stir in bean sprouts. Mix together soy sauce, lemon juice, sherry and ginger and pour over all. Place on serving dish and sprinkle with egg strips and tops of green onions. Serves 4. PER SERVING: 140 CALORIES, 5 GRAMS FAT.

NOTE: To expand this into a main dish, add protein such as 1 cup of cooked chopped chicken or thin strips of turkey ham and heat through.

PIZZA

>1 package dry yeast
>1 cup warm water
>1 teaspoon sugar
>2½ cups white flour
>1 teaspoon salt

Dissolve yeast in ¼ cup warm water, add sugar and let stand for 10 minutes. Add remaining water, flour and salt and beat very well until dough is completely smooth. Dough will be sticky but no kneading is required. Place dough in bowl sprayed with non-stick cooking spray, turn to coat the surface. Cover and let rise until doubled, about 1 hour.

Divide dough in half and let stand 10 minutes. Dough will be very elastic. Roll out into two 8 inch circles. Cover with chosen toppings. (See below.)

PIZZA TOPPINGS

>1½ cups tomato sauce
>½ teaspoon salt
>¼ teaspoon garlic powder
>¼ teaspoon dried oregano
>½ teaspoon dried basil
>½ teaspoon dried thyme
>¼ pound lean ground beef
>¼ cup finely chopped onion
>¼ cup finely chopped green pepper
>3 ounces sliced turkey ham
>½ cup sliced mushrooms
>few black olives, if necessary!
>¾ cup grated part-skim mozzarella cheese
>¼ cup grated cheddar cheese
>¼ cup grated Parmesan cheese

Heat tomato sauce, add salt and herbs and cook for 15 minutes until thickened slightly. Spread half the sauce on top of each pizza. Prepare fillings.

BEEF, ONION AND PEPPER TOPPING: Brown the lean beef under the broiler until fat has cooked out. Break into small chunks. Distribute meat evenly on top of one pizza, over sauce. Sprinkle raw onion and green pepper over top.

HAM AND MUSHROOM: Cut the turkey ham slices into 8 wedges each. Arrange in radiating rows on one pizza. Sprinkle mushrooms on top. Add a few chopped black olives if you must!

Mix together the mozzarella, cheddar and Parmesan cheese. Sprinkle evenly over both pizzas.

At this point you can cover the pizza and set aside in refrigerator to retard further rising.

Remove from refrigerator and let warm to room temperature ½ hour before cooking. Bake at 500 degrees for 8-10 minutes. Makes 2 pizzas, 6 servings each. PER SERVING: 160 CALORIES, 3.5 GRAMS FAT.

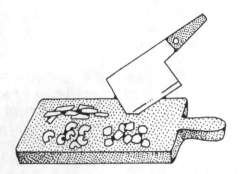

EGG FOO YUNG

    1 teaspoon oil
    ½ cup bean sprouts
    ¼ cup diagonally sliced green onion
    ¼ cup chopped celery
    ¼ cup chopped water chestnuts
    1 cup tiny cooked shrimp
    2 eggs + 1 egg white
    1 tablespoon soy sauce
    1 tablespoon sherry
    ¼ cup beef broth
    1 teaspoon cornstarch

Heat oil in large non-stick skillet or wok and stir-fry all vegetables until crisp-tender. Add shrimp and heat for 1 minute. Beat eggs and pour over vegetable-shrimp mixture, tilting pan so eggs cover everything. Cook until set.

Meanwhile, in separate pan, mix together soy sauce, sherry, broth and cornstarch and boil until thick and smooth. Divide egg foo yung into two servings and pour sauce equally over both portions. Serves 2. PER SERVING: 225 CALORIES, 9 GRAMS FAT.

BOMBAY CHICKEN SALAD

2 cups cooked chicken
4 ounces water chestnuts
½ cup diced celery
½ pound seedless green grapes
½ cup Mock Sour Cream, p. 170
¼ cup lowfat mayonnaise
1 teaspoon curry powder
1 teaspoon soy sauce
1 teaspoon lemon juice

Cut chicken into 1 inch cubes. Mix together chicken, water chestnuts and celery. OPTIONAL: At this time, you can blend the mixture briefly in the food processor to get a salad with a finer consistency, if desired.

Blend together the Mock Sour Cream, mayonnaise, curry powder, soy sauce and lemon juice. Pour over the chicken mixture. Stir in grapes. Chill several hours. Serves 6. PER SERVING: 150 CALORIES, 6 GRAMS FAT.

This salad improves with age and ingredient amounts can be adjusted to taste or to whatever you have on hand!

CHINESE CHICKEN SALAD

1 cup cooked chicken
½ cup water chestnuts
½ cup bean sprouts
½ cup chopped celery
¼ cup chopped green onion
1 cup cooked brown rice
2 tablespoons lowfat Italian dressing
1 teaspoon soy sauce
1 tablespoon lowfat mayonnaise
1 tablespoon Mock Sour Cream, p. 170
1 tablespoon lemon juice

In a large bowl, mix together chicken, water chestnuts, sprouts, celery and green onion. In a separate bowl, pour Italian dressing over the cooked rice and stir until absorbed, then add to the chicken mixture.

Mix together soy sauce, mayonnaise, Mock Sour Cream and lemon juice and toss with all other ingredients. Makes about 4 cups. PER CUP: 135 CALORIES, 3 GRAMS FAT.

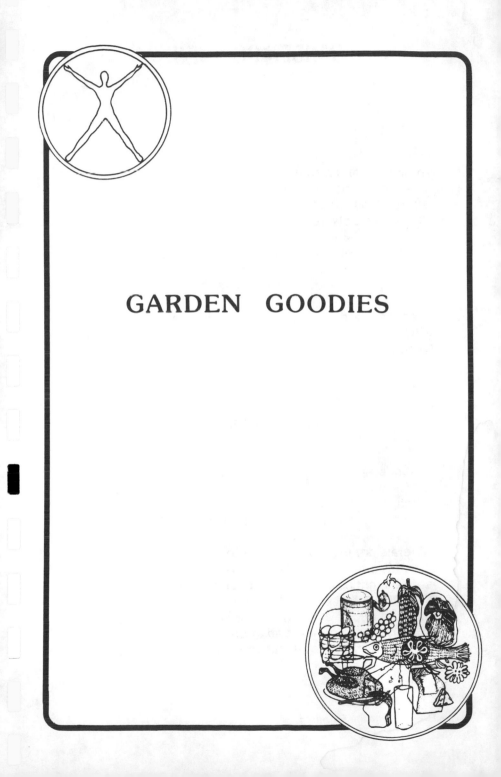

GARDEN GOODIES

GARDEN GOODIES

ABOUT VITAMINS

The word vitamin comes from the word "vital". Vitamins have no caloric value but are important to the body as "spark plugs" or enzymes that play an important role in all the metabolic reactions.

There are about twenty substances active as vitamins in human nutrition and when we eat a well balanced diet we get all we need for daily existence.

Vitamins are described as fat soluble (A, D, E and K), which are easily stored by the body, and water soluble (B and C), which are not stored.

ABOUT MINERALS

Minerals are important constituents of bones, teeth, soft tissue, muscle, blood and nerve cells. They help to maintain the fluid balance in the body, preventing blood and tissues from being too acid or too alkaline.

Minerals are usually divided into two categories, major minerals and trace minerals. Major minerals present in large quantities in the body include calcium, potassium, sodium and magnesium. Minerals important to our body but necessary only in trace amounts include iron, copper, zinc, flourine and manganese. Minerals are supplied by the food we eat and a balanced diet supplies all we need.

VEGETABLE COOKING

You will note that we have not included a lot of vegetable recipes — not because we don't like vegetables but frankly because we find it hard to improve on vegetables that are LIGHTLY STEAMED AND SERVED WITH FRESH LEMON SQUEEZED OVER THEM. This crisp, clean taste beats elaborate sauces and has no added fat!

This salad improves with time and can be kept refrigerated up to 3 days.

GARDEN TABOULI

½ cup bulgar
½ cup chicken broth
3 tablespoons lemon juice
1 tablespoon oil
¼ teaspoon garlic powder
¼ teaspoon dried oregano
½ cup canned kidney beans, drained
½ cup grated carrot
½ cup finely chopped green pepper
½ cup minced parsley
½ cup chopped tomatoes
½ cup chopped green onions
½ cup cucumber, peeled, seeded and chopped

Stir bulgar into chicken broth and let stand 30 minutes to soften. Mix together lemon juice, oil, garlic and oregano. Pour over bulgar.

Add all other ingredients, except cucumber, to bulgar, stir to mix well and chill a minimum of 1 hour. Add cucumber just before serving. Serves 4. PER SERVING: 240 CALORIES, 5 GRAMS FAT.

The sharp, refreshing taste of this salad enhances many main dishes. Buy the best virgin (or extra virgin) olive oil you can afford — the better the oil, the less you need for flavor!

LIGHT LETTUCE SALAD

    1 head tender leaf lettuce
    2 tablespoons VIRGIN olive oil (important!)
    ¼ teaspoon salt
    2 tablespoons lemon juice

Wash lettuce and dry thoroughly. Toss lettuce first with olive oil, sprinkle lightly with salt, then add the lemon juice and toss until well mixed. Serves 4. Calories and fat grams are basically from the oil. PER SERVING: 120 CALORIES, 7 GRAMS FAT.

JELLIED CLAMATO SALAD

    1 package unflavored gelatin
 1¾ cups Clamato (tomato/clam cocktail)
    2 tablespoons vinegar
    ½ cup tiny cooked shrimp
    ½ cup chopped celery
    ¼ cup diced avocado
    ¼ cup chopped green onion
      Mock Sour Cream as garnish, p. 170

Boil Clamato, pour over gelatin in large bowl. Stir in vinegar and cool until syrupy. Add shrimp (same a few for garnish) and vegetables and mix well. Pour into a 4" x 8" loaf pan. Chill until firm. Unmold or cut out individual servings. Serve on lettuce leaf with a dab of Mock Sour Cream on top; garnish with reserved shrimp. Serves 4.

MIXED VEGETABLE SALAD

1 16 ounce can green beans
1 16 ounce can wax beans
1 16 ounce can garbanzo beans
1 8 ounce can water chestnuts
4 thinly sliced carrots
½ cup sliced green onions
   lowfat yogurt
   dried dill to taste

Drain the beans and mix with other ingredients. Blend with a dressing made of lowfat yogurt to which you have added lots of dill! This recipe can be varied by adding or deleting various combinations of vegetables. Serves as many as you want!

CORN WITH ONIONS AND PEPPERS

1 teaspoon oil
½ cup finely chopped onion
1 clove minced garlic
1 cup finely chopped green pepper
2 cups whole kernel corn
½ teaspoon ground cumin
   salt and pepper to taste

Heat the oil in a skillet and add the onion, garlic and chopped pepper. Add corn, cumin, salt and pepper. Stir briefly, cover and cook over low heat about 3 minutes. Serves 4. PER SERVING: 80 CALORIES, 1 GRAM FAT.

NOTE: When fresh corn is in season, cut and scrape the kernels from 4 large ears (2 cups), then proceed as above.

ZUCCHINI FRITTERS

1 cup grated zucchini
2 eggs
6 tablespoons flour
½ teaspoon baking powder
¼ teaspoon salt

Drain the grated zucchini very well, add eggs and dry ingredients. Heat a non-stick frying pan and drop approximately 1 tablespoon of batter in pan for each fritter. Brown quickly, turn over to brown other side, remove from pan and keep warm until all are cooked. Serves 2. PER SERVING: 180 CALORIES, 7 GRAMS FAT.

ZUCCHINI-MUSHROOM CASSEROLE

¼ pound sliced mushrooms
1 teaspoon oil
2 cups grated zucchini
¼ teaspoon salt
¼ teaspoon garlic powder
⅛ teaspoon dried oregano
2 tablespoons grated Parmesan cheese
2 eggs, beaten very well

Brown mushrooms in oil, stir in all other ingredients, pour into a 1 quart baking dish sprayed with cooking spray. Bake at 350 degrees for 25 minutes. Serves 4. PER SERVING: 75 CALORIES, 5 GRAMS FAT.

ABOUT RICE AND BULGAR

Rice is one of the most underrated foods in our diet today. It adds fiber to our diet and fills us up without adding a lot of additional calories or fat.

WHITE RICE: Quick-cooking, with a bland flavor, white rice complements many meals.   Add a teaspoon of lemon juice to the water before you cook rice to keep it whiter and avoid stickiness.

BROWN RICE: If you haven't tried it you're missing a taste treat. It has a nutty flavor, as different from white rice as whole wheat bread is different from white. It contains more of the bran, therefore provides more vitamins and fiber. Brown rice takes longer to cook than white rice but if you can adjust your cooking schedule you may find it is very addictive!

BULGAR or cracked wheat is a grain that can be used as a substitute for rice. Unfortunately, bulgar seems to have the reputation of being used only in exotic mid-Eastern dishes (which we probably don't eat often) or as a breakfast cereal (in fact, it is usually found in the hot cereal section of supermarkets).

When bulgar is cooked very simply, as one would cook rice, it becomes a delicious, quickly prepared substitute for rice or potatoes. It is not necessary to make a pilaf by cooking it in chicken broth and it is certainly not necessary (nor desirable) to cook it first in butter and oil before adding the liquid. See the following recipe.

BROWN RICE RISOTTO

1 cup brown rice
¼ cup chopped onion
½ teaspoon dried thyme
¼ teaspoon salt
2 cups chicken broth
½ cup diced fresh mushrooms

Add brown rice, onion, thyme and salt to 2 cups chicken broth, bring to a boil, reduce heat, cover and simmer 30 minutes. Add diced mushrooms and continue cooking, covered, until all liquid is absorbed and rice is tender, about 45 minutes. Serves 4. PER SERVING: 200 CALORIES, 1 GRAM FAT.

BULGAR PILAF

1 teaspoon oil
¼ pound sliced mushrooms
¼ cup chopped green onions
1 clove minced garlic
1 cup bulgar
½ teaspoon salt
2 cups chicken broth

Heat oil and brown mushrooms, green onions and garlic briefly. Stir in bulgar, salt and chicken broth. Bring to a boil, cover and simmer for 20 minutes or until bulgar is tender. Serves 4. PER SERVING: 250 CALORIES, 2 GRAMS FAT.

BASIC BULGAR

1 cup bulgar or cracked wheat
2 cups water
½ teaspoon salt

Add the bulgar to boiling, salted water, immediately lower heat, cover and simmer about 15 minutes or until grains are tender but still slightly chewy. All the water should be absorbed. Serve anytime you would serve rice. Serves 4. PER SERVING: 150 CALORIES, LESS THAN 1 GRAM FAT.

CURRIED POTATO PATTIES

2 cups hot mashed potatoes
1 egg
¼ teaspoon curry powder
1 teaspoon chopped parsley

Place the hot mashed potatoes in a mixing bowl, add the egg, curry powder and parsley. Blend well and shape into 4 patties and place on a baking sheet sprayed with cooking spray.

Bake in a 400 degree oven for 10 minutes or until heated through. Serves 4. PER SERVING: 75 CALORIES, 2 GRAMS FAT.

Potatoes are good for you — it's only when you combine them with such extras as gobs of butter and sour cream that they become high-fat "no-no's".

SCALLOPED POTATOES

>   2 medium sliced potatoes (2 cups)
>   ½ cup chopped onion
>   ¼ cup chopped green pepper
>   ¼ teaspoon dried dill
>   1 teaspoon salt
>   1 tablespoon margarine
>   3 tablespoons flour
>   1½ cups 2% milk
>   ¼ cup grated sharp cheddar cheese

Spray a 1½ quart baking dish with cooking spray. Make alternating layers of potatoes, onions and green pepper, sprinkling dill and salt over each potato layer.

Melt margarine and drizzle over vegetables. Shake flour and milk together until smooth, stir in grated cheese and pour over the potato mixture.

Bake at 350 degrees for 1½ hours or until potatoes are tender when pierced with a fork. Cover the dish for the first 45 minutes, remove the cover for the remainder of the cooking. Serves 4. PER SERVING: 160 CALORIES, 7 GRAMS FAT.

NOTE: The addition of thin slices of turkey ham, at 35 calories and 1½ grams of fat per ounce, turns this into a supper casserole.

These are great with cabbage rolls for supper or as a brunch dish with applesauce and a slice of baked turkey ham.

RON'S SUNDAY-BEST POTATO PANCAKES

½ medium onion
¼ cup milk
2 large eggs
1 teaspoon salt
2 small baking potatoes (about 1½ cups)
¼ cup flour
¼ teaspoon baking powder

Blend onion and milk very thoroughly in blender. Add eggs and salt, blend well. Peel potatoes, cut into chunks and add to blender. Add flour on top of potatoes, then sprinkle baking powder on top of flour. After several short bursts to mix ingredients, blend at high speed for about 5 seconds. DO NOT OVERBLEND — you want a coarse but not lumpy mixture.

For each pancake, put 2 tablespoons potato mixture into hot, nearly smoking, non-stick pan and spread the batter very thin with the back of a small measuring cup or spoon. THIS IS IMPORTANT. Potatoes must be thin so they will cook quickly.

Flip once to brown both sides, remove and keep warm in oven until all are done. Leftovers can be reheated in a hot griddle the next day. Serves — — ? Hard to say! Two or three people can go through this batch easily. PER 1/3 RECIPE: 160 CALORIES, 5 GRAMS FAT.

NOTE: The amount of onion is to taste; amount of flour or milk may have to be adjusted depending on how watery the potatoes are. Batter should be thick but "pourable". Hard to describe but practice makes perfect!

PASTA

Pasta is a wonderful treat! It's really filling and is usually low in fat and high in fiber. We like pasta almost as much as chocolate chip cookies...especially since we began experimenting with various ways to cook it!

Here's a basic recipe that you can modify a hundred different ways: Fresh pasta (whole wheat is terrific), your choice of vegetables, some meat, chicken or shellfish, yogurt and/or Mock Sour Cream and/or lowfat mayonnaise.

For example: cook a sufficient amount of pasta for the appropriate number of servings. Meanwhile, in a microwave or non-stick pan, stir-fry the vegetable(s) of your choice (onions and mushrooms are a favorite combination) and some meat. When the pasta is done, add the vegetables and meat to it, with some appropriate spices to match, then add the milk-based product of your choice to cream it up. Voila! A quick and delicious meal with all four food groups represented.

Try pasta, boneless breast of chicken, mushrooms and dill.
pasta, Florida bay scallops, scallions and Italian seasoning.
pasta, yogurt, Parmesan cheese.
pasta, tuna, peas and onions, yogurt and lowfat mayonnaise.
pasta shells stuffed with tuna or chicken salad.
pasta with spaghetti sauce and mushrooms.

Use your imagination and your taste buds and you'll find that pasta is a winner, especially when it's cooked the lowfat way!

SAUCES

SAUCES

Mock Sour Cream can be used for a variety of purposes — as a base for cold sauces, as a dip with spices added, as a replacement for mayonnaise in salads, as a "bread spread" on a sandwich.

MOCK SOUR CREAM

> 1 cup lowfat cottage cheese
> ¼ cup lowfat yogurt
> 1 teaspoon lemon juice

Place cottage cheese in strainer, rinse under running water and drain well. Put cottage cheese in blender or food processor and add yogurt and lemon juice. Blend very well until completely smooth. Texture will be creamy.

Chill well. With fresh ingredients this will keep up to two weeks in the refrigerator. PER TABLESPOON: 15 CALORIES, 0.3 GRAMS FAT.

Try this on your family without telling them what it is and wait for enthusiastic comments!

MUSTARD-MAYO CREAM

Mix equal parts of Mock Sour Cream and Dijon mustard. Use in place of mustard and mayonnaise on sandwiches. PER TABLESPOON: 14 CALORIES, 0.5 GRAMS FAT.

Keep this mixture chilled as it has a softer consistency than regular cream cheese. It improves with 1-2 days aging. Use it whenever you want a cream cheese treat.

WHIPPED COTTAGE CREAM CHEESE

¾ cup lowfat cottage cheese
3 ounces Neuchatel cream cheese

Rinse the cottage cheese in a strainer and press out any excess moisture (IMPORTANT). Place in a blender with cream cheese and blend until smooth and creamy. Makes approximately 1 cup. Per tablespoon: 25 CALORIES, 1.5 GRAMS FAT.

NOTE: Per tablespoon, Neuchatel cream cheese has 35 calories and 3.5 grams fat; regular cream cheese has 50 calories and 5 grams fat.

BLUE CHEESE DRESSING

1 package dry ranch-style dressing mix
1 cup lowfat yogurt
1 cup buttermilk
¼ cup crumbled blue cheese

Blend together the packaged dip mix, yogurt and buttermilk until smooth. Stir in the crumbled blue cheese and refrigerate for at least 4 hours to blend flavors.

The dressing can be thinned out with more buttermilk, if desired. Makes about 2 cups. PER TABLESPOON: 7 CALORIES, 0.2 GRAMS FAT.

These sauces freeze beautifully and are very handy to have around, especially in the winter when you want a fresh tomato taste. Substitute Basic Tomato Sauce in any recipe calling for canned tomato sauce.

BASIC TOMATO SAUCE

      3 chopped onions
      1 chopped green pepper
      2 cloves minced garlic
      1 tablespoon oil
    10 cups fresh chopped tomatoes
      1 tablespoon salt
      1 teaspoon oregano
      2 bay leaves
      1 teaspoon dried basil

VERSION 1: Brown onion, green pepper and garlic in oil. Peel, seed and chop tomatoes and add to cooked vegetables, along with seasoning. Simmer until thick, about 2-3 hours. This sauce will be CHUNKY.

VERSION 2: Brown vegetables as above and add coarsely chopped tomatoes, not peeled or seeded. Simmer 2 hours, then force entire mixture through a food mill to remove seeds, skin and vegetable chunks. This sauce will be a SMOOTH puree. You may want to put it back into the pot and cook it until it is even thicker — another 2 hours won't hurt, just be careful it doesn't burn!

VERSION 3: Chop tomatoes coarsely. Do not peel or seed, just press through food mill, then add to previously browned vegetables. This results in a SMOOTH tomato sauce with SMALL CHUNKS of onion and green pepper.

FAVORITE CHILE SAUCE

8 pounds ripe tomatoes
4 sweet peppers (mix of red and green best)
1 stalk celery
2 cups chopped onions
2 cloves minced garlic
1 teaspoon whole allspice
1 teaspoon whole mustard seed
1 teaspoon whole cloves
1 cup brown sugar
1 teaspoon pepper
1 teaspoon dry mustard
1 tablespoon salt
2 dried, hot peppers, crushed
2 cups cider vinegar

Peel and seed tomatoes, cut in coarse chunks. Add to large pot with vegetables, simmer 45 minutes. Place whole spices in cheesecloth bag, add to tomatoes along with sugar, pepper, mustard, salt and hot peppers. Bring to a boil and simmer until thick. Add vinegar and continue cooking until desired thickness. Makes about 8 pints.

CUCUMBER SAUCE

½ cup shredded cucumber
½ cup Mock Sour Cream, p. 170
1 tablespoon chopped chives
1 tablespoon chopped green onion
1 tablespoon lemon juice
¼ teaspoon salt

Peel and seed the cucumber before shredding. Blot very dry with paper towel before adding rest of ingredients. Mix all together, chill well. Excellent with broiled fish. Makes about one cup. PER RECIPE: 150 CALORIES, 3 GRAMS FAT.

YOGURT-DILL SAUCE

1 cup lowfat yogurt
½ teaspoon dried dill
½ teaspoon Dijon mustard
½ cup chopped green pepper
½ cup chopped green onion, including tops

Mix all together, chill well. Serve with fish. Makes one cup. PER RECIPE: 145 CALORIES, 4 GRAMS FAT.

BREAD and BREAKFAST

BREAD AND BREAKFAST

ABOUT CARBOHYDRATES

The word "carbohydrate" breaks down to "carbo" (from carbon) and "hydra" (from water). Since water is made up of hydrogen and oxygen it is easy to see that carbohydrates are composed of the elements carbon, hydrogen and oxygen.

Carbohydrates are our most maligned food source. They provide 4 calories per gram and are the source for much of our body's energy needs.

Foods high in carbohydrates are the primary source of fiber in the diet. High carbohydrate foods such as whole grains and fresh fruits and vegetables are excellent low calorie, high fiber food sources. These foods also have a high satiety value — they give us a feeling of "fullness".

There are two kinds of carbohydrates, simple and complex. Simple carbohydrates are sugars that are easily broken down by the digestive system for quick utilization as energy sources. When you think of simple sugars think of the words that end in "—ose", such as glucose, fructose and galactose (the monosaccharides) and sucrose, lactose and maltose (the disaccharides). Examples include refined sugars and the naturally found sugars in fruits, milk and peas. The simple sugars that are refined, such as white table sugar, have little or no vitamin or mineral content and are considered to be "empty calories".

Complex carbohydrates require more enzymatic action by the digestive juices to be broken down for absorption and utilization by the body and contain many essential vitamins and minerals. These are the starches and fiber we eat as breads, rice, potatoes, cereals, fruits and vegetables.

U.S. DIETARY GOALS RECOMMEND A DIET IN WHICH UP TO 55% OF THE CALORIES ARE CARBOHYDRATES.

BREAD BAKING TIPS

Flour substitutions are easily made — experiment with whole wheat, rye, graham flours, etc. Health food stores carry a huge variety of cereals which are excellent in bread — 7 grain cereal, cracked wheat, oat bran. ¼ cup of raw bran or wheat germ adds nourishment to the finished product without changing the taste. Just make equal substitutions for regular flour.

As the amount of white flour decreases, the bread gets heavier and coarser. 100% whole grain bread will be delicious but rather solid! You may prefer to have at least ½ to ⅔ white flour. Also, if using any crunchy addition such as cracked wheat, soak it first in an equal amount of hot water until soft or your bread will be damaging to your teeth!

The amount of flour to be added when kneading is hard to predict, so the total may vary from that given in the recipe. The general rule is to keep the last half cup of flour for kneading, sprinkle it lightly on your kneading surface and work it in well until dough is not sticky.

Many of these recipes feature buttermilk for an extra tangy flavor. Feel free to use plain skim milk if you prefer.

SUPER GRAIN BREAD

1 package active dry yeast
½ cup lukewarm water
2 tablespoons molasses
2 tablespoons honey
1 tablespoon oil
1 cup buttermilk or skim milk
¾ cup whole wheat flour
¾ cup rye flour
¼ cup rolled oats (not instant)
¼ cup cornmeal
1 teaspoon salt
2 cups white flour (or more)

Mix yeast, water, molasses, honey and oil. Add buttermilk and stir well, making sure yeast is completely dissolved. Add whole wheat flour, rye flour, oats, cornmeal, salt and 1 cup of white flour. Stir 50 times.

Cover, let rise in warm place until doubled, about 1½ hours. Sprinkle board with ¾ cup white flour and knead into dough, adding more flour if dough is still sticky. When all flour has been absorbed, knead 200 times.

Shape into loaf, put in 4" x 8" pan sprayed with cooking spray. Cover and let rise in warm place until doubled, about 45 minutes.

Bake bread at 400 degrees for 20 minutes, then lower temperature to 350 degrees for 30 minutes longer. PER LOAF: 2000 CALORIES, 24 GRAMS FAT.

This loaf is "sturdy", slightly coarse and delicious!

MULTIGRAIN BUTTERMILK BREAD

1 package active dry yeast
¼ cup warm water
2 tablespoons brown sugar
1 tablespoon oil
¾ cup buttermilk
1 teaspoon salt
¼ teaspoon baking soda
¼ cup wheat germ
¼ cup raw bran
½ cup rye flour
1 cup whole wheat flour
1 cup white flour

Dissolve yeast in warm water, along with brown sugar. Add oil, buttermilk, salt and baking soda. Stir to mix well. Add wheat germ, raw bran and rye flour, stir vigorously to blend. Add whole wheat flour and mix well. Add white flour gradually.

Dough will be very stiff — the last half of the white flour may have to be added while kneading. Knead until dough is smooth and elastic. Turn into bowl sprayed with cooking spray, cover and let rise until doubled, about 2 hours.

Punch down, form into loaf and place in sprayed 4" x 8" pan. Cover and let rise again until doubled, about 1 hour.

Bake at 375 degrees 30 to 35 minutes. PER LOAF: 1500 CALORIES, 22 GRAMS FAT.

ONION DILL BATTER BREAD

1 package active dry yeast
¼ cup water
½ cup cottage cheese, blended smooth
½ cup lowfat yogurt
1 tablespoon oil
1 egg
½ teaspoon onion powder
1 teaspoon dill
½ teaspoon salt
¼ teaspoon baking soda
2½ cups flour

Dissolve yeast in warm water. Blend together smooth cottage cheese, yogurt, oil and egg. Add onion powder, dill and salt and stir well. Add dissolved yeast, baking soda and 1 cup of flour and stir vigorously for 2 minutes. Beat in remaining flour until dough is very stiff.

Place the dough in a bowl sprayed with cooking spray, cover and let rise until doubled in size (about 1 hour). Stir the dough down, turn out onto floured board and form into loaf — dough will be soft but can be patted out with the hands and rolled into shape. Place in 4" x 8" loaf pan that has been sprayed with cooking spray, cover and let rise until doubled again, about 45 minutes.

Bake at 350 degrees for 35 minutes. Cool on wire rack.
PER LOAF: 1400 CALORIES, 28 GRAMS FAT.

NO KNEAD, NO FAT LOAF!

1 package active dry yeast
¼ cup warm water
1 teaspoon sugar
1 teaspoon salt
1 cup skim milk
2½ cups white flour
¼ teaspoon baking soda
   cornmeal

Mix yeast with warm water and sugar, let stand for 5 minutes. When yeast is softened, add salt and milk. Stir in 1 cup of flour to which the baking soda has been added. Beat well for 2 minutes. Stir in rest of flour to make a stiff batter.

Spoon into 4" x 8" loaf pan that has been sprayed with cooking spray and sprinkled with cornmeal. Sprinkle top with cornmeal. Cover, let rise in warm place for 45 minutes or until doubled.

Bake at 400 degrees for 25 minutes. PER LOAF: 1100 CALORIES, 4 GRAMS FAT.

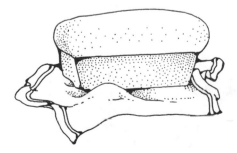

TRITICALE LOAF

½ cup boiling water
½ cup triticale flakes
1 package active dry yeast
¼ cup warm water
1 tablespoon oil
¼ cup honey
½ cup skim milk
1 teaspoon salt
1¼ cups white flour
¾ cup triticale flour
¼ cup wheat germ
¾ cup whole wheat flour

Pour boiling water over triticale flakes and set aside to soften and cool. Dissolve yeast in warm water, stir in oil, honey and skim milk. Add salt, white flour, triticale flour, wheat germ and cooled triticale flakes. Stir well then beat for 5 minutes. Gradually add whole wheat flour until stiff dough results. Turn out onto board floured with whole wheat flour and knead for 10 minutes, adding more flour as necessary to avoid sticking. Spray bowl with cooking spray, place dough in bowl, cover and let rise in warm place until doubled, about 1½ hours. Punch down, shape into loaf, place in loaf pan sprayed with cooking spray, cover and let rise until almost doubled, about 45 minutes. Bake at 350 degrees for 40 minutes or until bread is brown and sounds hollow when tapped. Remove from pan and cool on rack before slicing. PER LOAF: 1800 CALORIES, 26 GRAMS FAT.

Triticale flakes and flour can be found in health food stores. Triticale is a hybrid grain of wheat and rye. It averages 28% higher protein than wheat and contains all the essential amino acids to make it a complete protein. Enjoy it with a bean soup!

Use the sharpest cheddar you can afford to enhance the subtle cheese flavor without adding more fat.

CANADIAN CHEDDAR LOAF

1 package dry yeast
¼ cup warm water
1 teaspoon sugar
1 tablespoon oil
¾ cup skim milk
½ cup lowfat yogurt
½ cup grated sharp cheddar cheese
1 teaspoon salt
1 cup white flour
2 cups whole wheat flour or triticale flour

Dissolve yeast in warm water with sugar. Stir in oil, milk, yogurt, cheese and salt. Add white flour and beat vigorously until well blended. Then stir in the whole wheat flour gradually until dough is very stiff.

Turn out onto floured board and knead for 5 minutes, adding more whole wheat flour if necessary. Place in a bowl sprayed with cooking spray, turning to grease top of dough. Cover and let rise until doubled, about 1½ hours. Punch down and form into loaf. Place in 4" x 8" loaf pan sprayed with cooking spray. Cover and let rise until doubled, about 45 minutes.

Bake at 375 degrees for 40 minutes. Makes 1 loaf.
PER LOAF: 1700 CALORIES, 40 GRAMS FAT.

NOTE: Using triticale flour instead of whole wheat flour will increase the high protein content of this bread.

Oat bran is a fine-grained hot cereal. It gives this bread a smoother texture than some other whole grain breads.

COUNTRY OAT 'N HONEY BREAD

½ cup oat bran cereal
1 cup boiling water
1 package dry yeast
2 tablespoons honey
¼ cup warm water
1 tablespoon oil
½ cup skim milk
1 teaspoon salt
3 cups white flour

Cook oat bran in boiling water for 5 minutes, set aside to cool. Add yeast and honey to ¼ cup warm water and let stand until yeast is dissolved. Add oil, milk, salt and 1 cup of flour, mixing well. Stir in the cooled bran, then add remaining flour until dough is stiff.

Turn out onto a floured board and knead for about 8 minutes. Spray a bowl with cooking spray, add dough, turn over to grease top, cover and let rise until doubled, about 1½ hours.

Punch down, then let rise a second time, about 45 minutes. After the second rising, turn dough out onto floured board and shape into loaf. Place in a 4" x 8" loaf pan which has been sprayed with cooking spray. Cover and let rise until doubled, about 30 minutes.

Bake at 375 degrees for about 40 minutes or until bread is brown. PER LOAF: 1600 CALORIES, 22 GRAMS FAT.

BULGAR-CORNMEAL LOAF

1 cup water
½ cup bulgar (cracked wheat)
1 package active dry yeast
¼ cup warm water
2 tablespoons honey
1 tablespoon oil
½ cup buttermilk
1 teaspoon salt
¼ cup cornmeal
¾ cup whole wheat
2 cups white flour

Heat water to boiling, add bulgar and cook about 10 minutes, until tender. Cool thoroughly. Meanwhile, dissolve yeast in warm water. Add honey, stir well and set aside for 5 minutes. Stir in oil, buttermilk, salt and cornmeal. Add whole wheat flour and stir well. Add white flour in ½ cup amounts, mixing well after each addition, until you have a non-sticky dough that you can handle. This dough will be quite stiff because of the bulgar.

Turn it out onto a floured board and knead about 8 minutes, adding flour as necessary. Place in a bowl lightly sprayed with cooking spray, turning once to grease top. Cover and let rise in a warm place until doubled in size, about 1½ hours.

Punch down dough and pat out with hands. Shape into a loaf and place in a 4" x 8" pan which has been sprayed with cooking spray. Cover and let rise until doubled, about 45 minutes.

Bake in a 400 degree oven for 15 minutes, then reduce heat to 350 degrees and continue baking for another 15 minutes or until bread is golden brown and sounds hollow when tapped. PER LOAF: 2000 CALORIES, 22 GRAMS FAT.

These freeze very well and are delicious with a big bowl of soup.

CHEESE MINI-LOAVES

    1 package active dry yeast
   ¼ cup warm water
    1 teaspoon sugar
   ¾ cup buttermilk
    1 tablespoon oil
   ¼ teaspoon onion powder
    1 teaspoon salt
    1 cup white flour
 1½ cups whole wheat flour
   ¾ cup shredded sharp cheddar cheese

Soften yeast in warm water, add sugar and let stand for 10 minutes. Add buttermilk, oil, onion powder and salt. Beat well. Gradually beat in flours until dough is stiff and sticky. Stir in ½ cup cheese and blend well.

Cover bowl and let rise in warm place until almost doubled, about one hour. Stir dough down and spoon equally into six 1 cup baking dishes sprayed with non-stick cooking spray. Cover and let rise until almost doubled, about 30 minutes.

Sprinkle with rest of cheese, bake in a 350 degree oven until golden brown, about 30 minutes. Remove from dishes and cool. Makes 6. PER MINI-LOAF: 255 CALORIES, 7 GRAMS FAT.

WHOLE WHEAT PICNIC LOAVES

    1 package dry yeast
    1½ cups warm water
    1 teaspoon salt
    1½ cups whole wheat flour
    2 cups white flour
    1 teaspoon salt
    1 egg white mixed with 1 teaspoon water

Soften yeast in ¼ cup warm water. Add remaining water, salt and whole wheat flour and stir vigorously until well mixed. Add white flour in ½ cup amounts until dough is stiff.

Turn out on a floured board and knead for about 5 minutes, until smooth and stretchy. More flour may be added at this time to avoid excessive stickiness. Place dough in a bowl sprayed with cooking spray and turn once to grease the top. Cover and let rise in a warm place until doubled, about 1½ hours. Punch dough down and let rise a second time until doubled, about 45 minutes. Punch dough down and turn out onto a floured board.

Divide dough into 4 equal pieces, roll each into a round ball and place on a non-stick cookie sheet sprinkled with cornmeal. Brush rolls with egg white/water mixture. Let rolls stand in a warm place until doubled, about 30 minutes. Do not cover the rolls — a towel would stick to the egg white!

Place a pan of hot water in the oven and preheat oven to 375 degrees. Leave the pan on a rack under the rolls during the baking period. When rolls are doubled, brush again with egg white glaze and bake for 30 minutes or until brown. Makes 4. PER LOAF: 350 CALORIES, 2 GRAMS FAT.

RAISIN-BRAN BREAD

> ½ cup rolled oats (not instant)
> 1 cup hot water
> 1 package active dry yeast
> ¼ cup warm water
> ¼ cup honey
> 1 tablespoon oil
> ½ cup buttermilk or skim milk
> ¼ cup wheat germ
> ½ cup raw bran
> 1 teaspoon salt
> 1 cup raisins
> 1 cup whole wheat flour
> 1½ cups white flour (or more)

Soften rolled oats by soaking in hot water for about 10 minutes. Let cool. Dissolve yeast in warm water. Add honey, oil, buttermilk, wheat germ, soft rolled oats, raw bran and salt. Stir vigorously. Add raisins, whole wheat flour and enough white flour to make a stiff dough.

Turn out onto floured board and knead until smooth and not sticky, about 5 minutes. Place in bowl sprayed with cooking spray, cover and let rise until doubled, about 1½ hours.

Punch down, form into loaf, place in 4" x 8" pan sprayed with cooking spray and let rise again until doubled, about 45 minutes.

Bake at 375 degrees for about 40 minutes. PER LOAF: 2100 CALORIES, 26 GRAMS FAT.

COTTAGE CHEESE PANCAKES

1 cup lowfat cottage cheese
½ cup skim milk
2 eggs
2 tablespoons sugar
½ teaspoon baking powder
½ cup flour

Blend all ingredients together until smooth. Heat a non-stick frying pan medium-hot and put in about 2 tablespoons of batter for each pancake. Brown quickly on one side, turn and brown the other side. Remove from pan and keep warm while cooking remaining pancakes. Serves 4. PER SERVING: 165 CALORIES, 4 GRAMS FAT.

NOTE: Try topping these with a mixture of yogurt and sliced fruit lightly sweetened to taste. Or mix 1 teaspoon of low-calorie jam with 2 tablespoons plain yogurt for a treat. Just a few calories and pure delight!

Give your day a good high protein start.

RICOTTA CHEESE PANCAKES

½ cup part-skim ricotta cheese
1 egg + 1 egg white
3 tablespoons flour
1 tablespoon sugar

Blend together ricotta cheese and eggs until smooth, stir in flour and sugar. Heat a non-stick frying pan medium-hot and use a large spoonful of batter for each pancake. Brown quickly on one side, turn and brown the other side. Keep warm while cooking remaining pancakes. Serves 2. PER SERVING: 190 CALORIES, 8 GRAMS FAT.

BLUEBERRY BUTTERMILK PANCAKES

1 cup buttermilk
1 egg + 1 egg white
1 tablespoon oil
1 cup flour
1 tablespoon sugar
1 teaspoon baking powder
½ teaspoon baking soda
½ teaspoon salt
1 cup blueberries, fresh or frozen

Beat together buttermilk, eggs and oil. Mix dry ingredients and add to milk mixture, blending well. Stir blueberries in gently. (If frozen, no need to thaw). Cook on medium-hot non-stick griddle until brown on both sides and firm to touch. Makes about 12 pancakes, 4 inches each. PER THREE CAKES: 200 CALORIES, 7 GRAMS FAT.

LEFTOVER BRAN MUFFINS?

Crumble them in a bowl with fruit such as bananas or berries, stir in lowfat yogurt lightly sweetened to taste. Nutritious, delicious and very quick!

SWEET TREATS

SWEET TREATS

ABOUT SUGAR

Do you think you could eat your weight in sugar? Well, if you are 120 pounds or under the chances are you do. Americans consume an average of 120 pounds of sugar a year. That computes to about 10 teaspooons of sugar daily. Of course we don't eat refined sugar out of the bowl in those quantities but the consumption of sugar in the American diet has increased since the turn of the century by almost 200%. Much of this increase has been brought about by the dramatic increase in the use of corn sweeteners and other sugars by food processors.

Sugar itself isn't any more fattening than other carbohydrates or proteins and it is half as fattening as the fats we eat. The problem is that sugar has so little nutrient density — it's an empty calorie doing nothing more for us than changing the character of the food we eat. In addition, a lot of sugar calories are often packed into very small portions of food, making us consume lots of extra calories before we fill up.

Be aware that many foods are touted as "health foods" because they use more "naturally occurring sugars". In fact, health snacks made from honey and peanut butter are not much different in terms of fat or caloric content than walnut dreams (butter and walnuts with powdered sugar)! Since honey is more likely to stick to our teeth and promote tooth decay we may even be worse off! The term "health food" is a common misnomer. The bottom line is that SUGAR IS SUGAR.

Now for the good news. Sugar is an essential energy source, so before we bury it under attack let's be sure we understand what the word means.

Sugar is a loose term used for many forms and sources of carbohydrates that are used in a variety of ways. Sucrose is the most common form of sugar and is supplied as white granulated sugar, brown sugar (white sugar moistened and flavored with molasses) and confectioners sugar, which is powdered white sugar with cornstarch added. Fructose, or levulose, occurs naturally in fruit or honey. Lactose in milk, sucrose in cane or beets and maltose in beer are all sugars. Glucose is the name given to blood sugar. No matter what the original source of the sugar is, the body eventually breaks it down to its useful form, glucose. Glucose is either used immediately as an energy source, stored in the liver as glycogen (an easily broken down product) or stored as fat.

To help you with shopping, here are some names under which many manufacturers hide the addition of sugar to their products:

Cane Sugar	Corn Syrup
Dextrose	Fructose
Honey	Invert Sugars
Lactose	Maltose
Molasses	Sorbitol

CHOCOLATE MOUSSE

1 tablespoon instant coffee
1 tablespoon boiling water
4 ounces semisweet chocolate
2 eggs + 1 egg white
4 tablespoons sugar
2 tablespoons brandy

Dissolve coffee in boiling water, add chocolate and melt slowly over very low heat. Let cool.

Separate eggs and beat the 3 egg whites until stiff. Set aside.

In a separate bowl but with the same beaters, beat the 2 egg yolks until thick, add sugar and beat until well dissolved.

Pour cooled chocolate/coffee mixture and brandy into egg yolks and stir until well mixed. Fold this mixture carefully into the beaten egg whites.

Fill 6 small dessert dishes and chill for 4 hours before serving. Serves 6. PER SERVING: 175 CALORIES, 8 GRAMS FAT.

SWEET TIP

You CAN re-educate your taste buds — cut down the sugar content in your recipes by one-third to one-half.

STRAWBERRY CREAM CHEESE PIE

CRUST:

1 cup crushed graham cracker crumbs
2 tablespoons melted butter

Mix together crumbs and butter until evenly moistened.
Pat into 7 inch pie plate and bake for 10 minutes at 350
degrees. Let cool.

FILLING:

1 envelope gelatin
¼ cup water
¼ cup Whipped Cottage Cream Cheese, p. 171
2 cups crushed strawberries
2 tablespoons sugar
3 egg whites
¼ cup heavy cream
2 tablespoons sugar

Soften gelatin in water, then bring to a boil to dissolve
it. Beat together gelatin, Whipped Cottage Cream
Cheese, crushed berries and 2 tablespoons sugar.

In separate bowl, beat egg whites until stiff. In another
bowl, whip cream until soft peaks form, then stir in
sugar.

Gently fold together the egg whites and whipped cream,
then fold this mixture carefully into the berry mixture.
Pour gently into the cooled pie shell and refrigerate
until firm. Serves 6. PER SERVING: 175 CALORIES,
10 GRAMS FAT.

LEMON SPONGE LAYER CAKE

    4 large eggs, separated
    ½ cup sugar
    2 tablespoons lemon juice
    1 teaspoon lemon peel, finely grated
    1 cup cake flour
    1 teaspoon baking powder
    ¼ teaspoon salt

Beat egg whites until frothy, add ¼ cup sugar, then beat until stiff but not dry. Set aside.

With same beaters, beat egg yolks until thick, add ¼ cup sugar, lemon juice and peel. Beat until well mixed.

Mix together flour, baking powder and salt and fold gently, by hand, into egg yolk batter. Then very gently fold egg whites into batter.

Pour into 9" x 13" inch layer pan which has been sprayed with cooking spray. Bake at 350 degrees for about 25 minutes or until golden and springy. Serves 12. PER SERVING: 95 CALORIES, 2 GRAMS FAT.

CAKE CRAVINGS

If a celebration is coming up and you yearn for a piece of cake, ANGEL FOOD CAKE is your best bet — no shortening, no egg yolks, no fat. (Follow a recipe from any general cookbook or buy a mix.) Your next best bet is a SPONGE CAKE — no shortening, some egg yolks, therefore some fat. (See Lemon Sponge Layer Cake recipe.) All other cakes have lots of fat to make them tasty!

TRIFLE

⅙ Lemon Sponge Layer Cake (4" x 5" piece)
¼ cup milk
½ cup drained canned peaches, water-packed
2 tablespoons cornstarch
2 tablespoons sugar
1 teaspoon vanilla
1½ cups milk
½ cup ricotta cheese
1 tablespoon sugar

Cut up cake into 1 inch cubes, press into bottom of 1 quart shallow bowl. Sprinkle with milk, then layer peaches over top.

Prepare a sauce by mixing together cornstarch and sugar, then adding milk. Bring to a boil, stirring constantly, and cook 1 minute or until thick. Add vanilla.

Beat ricotta cheese and sugar until smooth, stir into sauce. Pour sauce over soaked cake and let stand in refrigerator several hours or overnight for flavors to blend. Serves 4. PER SERVING: 195 CALORIES, 6 GRAMS FAT.

NOTE: Lightly crushed berries sweetened to taste can be substituted for peaches. Cake can be sprinkled with 1 — 2 tablespoons orange liqueur in addition to the milk.

Try this easy, lowfat version of a traditional treat — don't expect it to taste the same — DO expect it to taste refreshing and delicious!

FAST FRUIT SHORTCAKE

For each serving, cut Lemon Sponge Layer Cake into 3 inch square pieces. Sprinkle each piece with 2 tablespoons skim milk so cake is "spongy" with milk. Top with generous serving of fruit, (fresh or barely thawed, if frozen) which has been sweetened to taste. Fruit suggestions: raspberries, strawberries, peaches, bananas.

FIBER-HIGH FRUIT MOUSSE

2 ripe bananas
1 lemon, pulp and juice
1 orange, pulp and juice
1 cup berries, fresh or frozen
1 cup lowfat yogurt
3 tablespoons sugar
1 envelope gelatin
½ cup water, divided

Blend all fruits together in blender or food processor. Add yogurt and sugar substitute. Blend until mixture is smooth.

Soften gelatin in ¼ cup cold water, then add ¼ cup boiling water to completely dissolve it. Add dissolved gelatin mixture to fruit and blend well. Pour into serving dish and chill until firm. Serves 6. PER SERVING: 105 CALORIES, 1 GRAM FAT.

BERRY PARFAIT

1 teaspoon gelatin
2 tablespoons cold water
2 pints fresh berries, divided
2 cups buttermilk
½ cup sugar, divided in half
½ teaspoon vanilla
2 egg whites

Soften gelatin in water and heat until dissolved. Blend 1 pint of berries smooth, combine with gelatin, buttermilk, ¼ cup sugar and vanilla. Freeze.

Beat whites until soft peaks form, then add remaining sugar and beat until stiff. Remove frozen berry mixture from freezer, beat briefly until smooth and fold into egg whites. Freeze.

To serve, remove from freezer and let soften about 15 minutes. Beat briefly and fill glasses with alternating layers of parfait and remaining berries, sliced. Serves 6. PER SERVING: 140 CALORIES, 0.2 GRAMS FAT.

SHERBET SMOOTHIE

½ cup orange sherbet
1 cup buttermilk
4 teaspoons sugar

Blend all together at highest speed and serve immediately in tall glasses. Serves 2. PER SERVING (with regular sherbet): 150 CALORIES, 1 GRAM FAT.

OVERCOMING

THE CHOCOLATE CHIP COOKIE BLUES

"A true story!"

I admit it! I'm a chocolate chip cookie junkie! In fact, I'm a chip junkie. I tried switching to carob chips and found I liked them to excess, also (as I did date chips and butterscotch chips and peanut butter chips)! You can put the little devils in anything and it's almost a guaranteed tasty food to my palate.

I knew it would be foolish to say 'I am NEVER going to eat a chocolate chip cookie again'. I would be setting myself up for defeat...and I deserved better! So what's a girl to do?

First of all, I made a pact with myself that I would never purchase chips to bring home and sit idly by, tempting me to eat them plain or in raw cookie dough. (Don't knock it if you haven't tried it!) (P.S. Don't try it!!)

Then I decided if I wanted to eat a chocolate chip cookie it should be the tastiest one in town. I set out on a careful study of chocolate chip cookies. You might think this would contribute to my demise, but it didn't because I laid out ground rules for the search. Never more than two experimental cookies a week — regardless of size.

I was surprised to learn that I could almost look at a chocolate chip cookie and determine if I would like it even before I bought it — it saved me lots of money. (I also now admit that I handled a couple in cookie jars and rejected them before they hit my face.)

I finally settled on two sources. Fortunately for me they were not convenient to get to and it worked successfully into my game plan that if I was going to eat a chocolate chip cookie it would be one of the favorites — and I would have to drive to get ONE cookie!

The second part of the plan was to find allies to my effort. What better choice than the salespeople? Despite a decrease in my purchases of chocolate chip cookies they have been very cooperative in helping with my cookie plan. And they're flattered to know that their cookies are "the best"!

I am not permitted to purchase more than one cookie at a time...no matter what excuse I come up with. (I once tried leaving the store, returning two minutes later and plea bargaining that it was a separate purchase...fortunately, I lost my case!) Chocolate chip cookies must be savored. When I finally get my one cookie, it lasts longer when I take a bite, put it down and come back later. (Oh, the power of that self discipline!). Well, it works for me.

R.G.

HOW WILL YOU HANDLE YOUR OWN
"CHOCOLATE CHIP COOKIE BLUES"?

SPICY GINGERCRISPS

    ½ cup margarine
    ⅔ cup sugar
    1 egg
    ¼ cup molasses
  1¾ cup flour
    1 teaspoon ground ginger
    1 teaspoon cinnamon
  1½ teaspoons baking soda
    ½ teaspoon salt
    ¼ cup sugar (approx.)

Beat together margarine and ⅔ cup sugar until creamy. Add egg and molasses and beat well. Mix together flour, ginger, cinnamon, baking soda and salt and add to creamed mixture, beating well.

Using 1 teaspoon of dough, roll it into a small ball, then roll lightly in the additional sugar. Place on a non-stick cookie sheet and bake at 350 degrees for 10 minutes. Makes 60. EACH: 45 CALORIES, 1.6 GRAMS FAT.

COOKIE COOKING TIP

Cookies are hard for most of us to pass up and unfortunately their fat content is what makes them so delicious. However, the simple trick of making your cookies SMALLER than usual will help you consume less fat. Most of us eat cookies by habit — one with a cup of coffee, a couple in our lunch bag, etc. If they're smaller, you'll still take the usual one or two — and get away with fewer calories and fat grams. Try it!

OATMEAL FLAKEROONS

½ cup margarine
½ cup brown sugar
½ teaspoon vanilla
1 egg
¾ cup flour
½ teaspoon baking soda
¼ teaspoon salt
¼ teaspoon cinnamon
1½ cups regular rolled oats

Cream margarine and sugar, add vanilla and egg and beat until smooth. Mix flour, baking soda, salt and cinnamon and add to creamed mixture. Beat well, then work in oatmeal. Batter will be very thick.

Roll dough into 1 inch balls and place on non-stick cookie sheet. Bake at 350 degrees for 12 to 15 minutes. Cool 1 minutes in pan before removing. Makes 40. EACH: 50 CALORIES, 2.5 GRAMS FAT.

PEANUT BUTTER OATMEAL COOKIES

¼ cup margarine
¼ cup peanut butter
¼ cup brown sugar
¼ cup white sugar
1 egg
¼ teaspoon vanilla
½ cup white flour
¼ teaspoon salt
¼ teaspoon baking soda
1 cup regular rolled oats

Cream together margarine, peanut butter and sugars. Add egg and vanilla and beat well. Add flour, salt and baking soda, mix well. Stir in oatmeal.

Form into 1 inch balls and place on non-stick cookie sheet. Press down with fork to ¼ inch thickness. Bake at 350 degrees for 10 minutes or until firm. Makes 60. EACH: 55 CALORIES, 2.6 GRAMS FAT.

PEACH YOGURT

2 cups sliced fresh peaches
1 teaspoon vanilla
1 cup lowfat yogurt
2 tablespoons sugar
2 egg whites
1 tablespoon gelatin
½ cup water, divided in half

Mix together peaches, vanilla, yogurt, sugar and egg whites.

Add gelatin to ¼ cup cold water to soften, then add ¼ cup boiling water to dissolve. Add dissolved gelatin to all other ingredients and beat well. The result will be a creamy mixture. Chill until soft set. Serves 6. PER SERVING: 65 CALORIES, 1 GRAM FAT.

TIPS AND TECHNIQUES
FOR THE LOWFAT LIFESTYLE

MEAL-PLANNING IDEAS

Here are some suggestions for using several of the recipes in this book. There are many more which fit in these categories. As you discover them, you might want to jot them down alongside the appropriate sections below.

COMPANY SPECIALS

Chicken Cannelloni, p. 126
Chicken Cordon Bleu, p. 125
Company Best Chicken Supremes, p. 122
Coquilles, p. 133
Creamy Cold Zucchini Soup, p. 75
Cream of Asparagus Soup, p. 74
Fisherman's Shellfish Stew, p. 137
Shrimp and Scallop Crepes, p. 140
Shrimps in a Pot, p. 136

QUICK AND EASY

Beef 'n Broccoli, p. 90
Chicken Chablis, p. 117
Chicken Chop Suey, p. 130
Chinese Chicken, p. 118
Confetti Chicken, p. 120
Not So Original Joe's Special, p. 98
Oriental Flank Steak, p. 81
Quick Devilled Fish, p. 134
Spring Chicken, p. 124
Stroganoff, p. 103

FAMILY DINNERS

Barbecued Beef, p. 86
Bottoms-Up Chowder, p. 139
Cabbage Rolls*, p. 100
Chicken Cacciatore, p. 128
Chile Swiss Steak*, p. 83
Lasagne, p. 107
Meal-Saver Meat Sauce*, p. 106
Mid-Week Manicotti*, p. 108
Oven-Baked Stew*, p. 85
Pizza, p. 152
Rib-Sticker Soup*, p. 66
Stuffed Flank Steak, p. 82
Tomato-Lentil Soup*, p. 73

   * Make ahead and freeze

BREAKFAST

Blueberry Buttermilk Cakes, P. 190
Cottage Cheese Pancakes, p. 189
Fast Frittata, p. 148
Potato Pancakes, p. 167
Ricotta Pancakes, p. 189
Sunday Special Omelet, p. 147

LUNCH

Bombay Chicken Salad, p. 155
Chinese Chicken Salad, p. 156
Crunchy Shrimp Salad Sandwich, p. 145
French Dip Sandwich, p. 146
French Onion Soup, p. 72
Simple 'Sam'-Wich, p. 144
Winter Vegetable Soup, p. 67
Tuna Alaska, p. 144

RULES FOR REPAST*

Don't eat unless you're hungry.

Stop eating when you feel satisfied.

Sit down at a table whenever you eat.

Prepare and serve your food attractively.

Learn to thoroughly taste and enjoy each bite of food.

Record everything you swallow.

Acquire a taste for snacking fiber foods instead of sweet foods.

Save your reading for non-eating hours.

If you usually head to the refrigerator when you enter the house, try coming in a different door to break the habit.

Avoid telephone conversations in the kitchen; it's too easy to nibble absentmindedly while you're talking.

Let someone else have the privilege of unloading groceries or cleaning up after meals if these are times when you succumb to nibbling.

*Repast = a meal   *Tips and Techniques*

Find alternatives to eating when you feel blue, sad, lonely, unloved or just generally depressed.

Find alternatives to eating when you feel happy, satisfied, lucky, pleased. Food is not the only appropriate way to celebrate an event.

Find a trusted friend who will support your new eating habits, be willing to hear from you during your weak moments and offer an encouraging word when you need it. Better yet, convert her to this new lifestyle!

ALTERNATE BEHAVIORS
TO INCREASE CALORIC OUTPUT

Embarking on a lifestyle that includes changes in the way you choose foods is a challenge that can be especially rewarding when combined with changes in your activity level that enable you to burn additional calories with the investment of only a small amount of additional time. There are many ways to increase daily energy expenditure. Try just one or two of the following suggestions, then add some of your own to get a more active outlook on the way you live.

When driving to work or taking public transportation, stop an increasingly longer distance from your work site and walk the remaining distance. Walking to and from a car or bus stop one-half mile away from work at a pace sufficient to make the body more efficient at burning body fat can burn the equivalent of seven pounds of fat in one year.

When travelling relatively short distances, walk instead of taking your car or the bus.

Use your lunch hour as an opportunity to participate in some kind of physical activity. Walking is an ideal way to finish any meal especially if you have the pleasure of good company or make a point to see the beauty of the world around you!

Get up a half hour early and take a walk, bicycle ride or swim before breakfast.

Replace your cocktail hour with 20 minutes of exercise.

Replace your coffee breaks with exercise breaks.

Walk up and down the stairs instead of using elevators.

Sweep the sidewalks and patios around your house or apartment regularly.

Gardening, mowing the lawn, washing the car are all excellent opportunities for exercise and muscle work. Replace any hired help and undertake some of these physical tasks yourself.

During television commercials run in place, walk up and down the stairs or do any other activity that blocks a trip to the kitchen for a snack.

Play golf without a golf cart or a caddy.

Don't be locked in to a daily routine that prevents you from modifying existing behaviors. A willingness to commit yourself to a new lifestyle that incorporates more vigorous activities within the framework of your daily routine will increase your caloric output and give you a more positive outlook.

LABELS — REQUIRED READING!

EATING MAY BE DANGEROUS TO YOUR GOOD HEALTH!

The husband of a former college roommate is a package designer with a formidable reputation. Some of the most familiar packages on our grocery shelves have been designed in his office and a visit there opened our eyes to the psychological role packaging has on our shopping selections.

Happily, he does not write the copy that appears on the food labels. Some of that is dictated by law, e.g. ingredients must be listed in their order of concentration in the package with the largest quantity first and the smallest quantity last.

U.S. government regulations also require that all EN-RICHED or FORTIFIED foods and those for which a nutrition claim is made must include information on the label.

It's somewhat amusing to see so many products advertised as "enriched" or "fortified", since it usually means that lots of vitamins have been added to replace the original nutrients which were removed in the processing of the product. For example, most white bread is called "enriched" when in fact there have been 22 nutrients removed from the flour through processing and 7 added back to give it some substance!

Dick (renowned food packager described above) does highlight nutrition information on labels because providing this information is very "in" right now. Consumers want to know more about what they are purchasing.

In fact, Madison Avenue copy writers have done an excellent job of disguising high amounts of sugar or fat in their packaged goods by disguising them with other names.

Sugars are often disguised by calling them by their official names! Anytime you see an ingredient that ends in the letter "—ose" you can be sure that it is a sugar. Some examples include: sucrose, (cane sugar), fructose (fruit sugar), dextrose (simple sugar). Other ways to describe sugar products are by calling them corn syrup, invert syrup, honey, molasses, natural sweeteners. If you see these products listed near the beginning of a label you can be sure the food has a high sugar content!

There are also other ways of describing fats on food labels. Some example include: vegetable salad oil, soybean oil, palm oil, etc. OILS ARE 100% FAT! A recent trip to a health food bakery once again reinforced our belief that most people know very little about food. When the salesperson was asked if a bread was low in fat, she said, "Oh yes, we use only the finest soybean oil in our bread — never any margarine or butter." FAT IS FAT IS FAT and you don't need a lot of it in food in order for it to be tasty!

AND THEN THERE ARE FOOD ADDITIVES...

Every year we consume more than four pounds of chemical preservatives, stabilizers, colorings, flavorings and other additives in our food.

Additives are purposely added to food for a variety of reasons. Like everything in life, there are good and bad reasons for adding chemical substances to food and there are food additives that are considered more or less desirable. Many convenience foods would not be available if preservatives and antioxidants weren't added to maintain product quality. Food additives also aid in the processing and preparation of foods and make many products more appealing in color and flavor.

Here's something else to think about. When there are nine food additives listed on one package and only one on a comparable package, it's not necessarily the latter that is the wisest choice. There may be only minute quantities of the additives in the first package and megadoses of the one additive in the second. Unfortunately, labelling has not become so informative that we can really be sure of what we're eating.

It is impossible to completely avoid food additives. Although there are indications that food additives may predispose us to some diseases, there are no clear medical or scientific studies that prove they are harmful to our health. If you have an aversion to these substances you can avoid convenience foods and eat foods as close to their natural state as possible.

We're back to the same old story, folks! Lots of fresh fruits and vegetables, whole grains and cereals and foods low in fat and sugar and high in fiber have very few food additives. Ah, give us the LOWFAT LIFE-STYLE any day!

Poor Dick. We told him what we thought of his labels. He wasn't even guilty — he just designed the package. But we've told him to tell the manufacturer that until he gives us the whole truth and nothing but the truth, we're not buying!

READ THE LABEL, PLEASE, READ THE LABEL.

Learn to start checking labels of processed food to find out the fat content as well as the calorie count in a serving. Most food packagers list the weight or volume of the package, the total number of calories and the number of calories per serving, then list the calories as grams.

It is also important to check the size of the serving. If it does not match what you usually eat or serve to your family, the numbers may be misleading.

Suppose you have a package of yogurt listing calories as grams of fat, grams of carbohydrate and grams of protein. You wish to know HOW MANY FAT CALORIES ARE IN EACH SERVING AND WHAT PERCENTAGE OF THE YOGURT IS FAT.

To determine the number of calories per gram use the following conversions:

> 1 gram of carbohydrate = 4 calories
>
> 1 gram of protein   = 4 calories
>
> 1 gram of fat   = 9 calories

1. Find the number of calories per serving (on label)

2. Find the number of grams of fat per serving (on label)

3. Convert the grams of fat to calories by multiplying by 9 (there are 9 calories in every gram of fat)

4. Find the percentage of fat calories per serving with the following formula:

$$\frac{\text{Number of fat calories}}{\text{Total calories}} = \% \text{ fat}$$

EXAMPLE: One 8 ounce container of yogurt

Total calories   = 200

Number of servings per container =   1

Number of calories per serving   = 200

Fat per serving   =   4 grams

CALCULATION:

4 grams x 9 calories per gram =
                        36 fat calories per serving

$$\frac{36 \text{ fat calories}}{200 \text{ total calories}} = 18\% \text{ fat}$$

A CAVEAT

Don't automatically assume that foods lower in fat are lower in calories. We found a brand of lowfat yogurt that had as many calories as another higher fat yogurt. The reason?   Those little manufacturing devils had concocted a recipe that added sugar to the yogurt, replacing the calories that had been removed with some of the fat. The unwary consumer then buys it, expecting it to be low in calories and healthy!

If YOUR favorite packaged goods — vegetables, soups, etc. — don't have nutritional information on the package label, take one minute to address a card to the manufacturer, saying, "I really like your product but I'm trying to be an informed consumer. I wish you'd put some nutritional information on your package. How about sending it to me so I can be assured that this product lives up to the high standards I want my family to enjoy." You're going to love their reply!

SHOPPING THE LOWFAT LIFESTYLE WAY

One of the major advantages of shopping for a diet low in fat, low in sugar and high in fiber is that it is less expensive than the normal American 45% fat diet! Chicken costs less than steak, fresh fruit beats store-bought pie and ice cream and a pot of bean soup can feed a family for pennies!

There are shopping tricks that are time-tested for lowering food bills and preventing unnecessary (and usually fattening) purchases. As you try to make some changes in the way you choose food you'll find modifying your shopping patterns will save you time, money and fat calories.

SHOP THE PERIMETER. Did you realize that supermarkets are laid out in a fashion designed to promote the purchase of the more profitable packaged goods stocked in the middle aisles? In addition to costing more, packaged goods generally contain more fat, more sugar, more preservatives and less fiber than the fresh foods stocked at the perimeter of the store. Wheel your grocery cart around the outer aisles and make only occasional trips to the "interior" for necessities such as tuna, pasta and whole grain cereal.

NEVER SHOP WHEN YOU ARE HUNGRY. The best time to go shopping for groceries is after you've had a satisfying, complete meal.

GO WITH A GROCERY LIST AND STICK TO IT. Blind yourself to the seduction of unnecessary food items. If prowling supermarkets is one of your stress reduction techniques (and for many people it is), move to the hardware, sundries or cosmetics sections. You'll be amazed at the little items there just waiting to be touched — and they have NO calories! It's a great place if you must satisfy impulse buying. Better to come home with a box of nuts and bolts than a box of cookies. Think of how righteous you'll feel!

TRY TO TAKE ONLY SUFFICIENT MONEY TO COVER THE PURCHASES YOU KNOW YOU NEED. In this era of check-writing, that's not always easy. If you intend to browse, first purchase and pay for your necessary items and carry them to the car. (You'll burn a few extra calories here.) Moving outside the store may be sufficient incentive to encourage you to spend your free time on a brisk aerobic walk! If you must return to the store, promise yourself that if you purchase any additional items you'll stand in the LONGEST CHECKOUT LINE. Making the purchase of unnecessary items difficult is the best way to prevent yourself from doing it.

MAKE FRIENDS WITH YOUR GROCERY CLERKS. These people can be your allies in your fight against fat. If you have a personal checkout person who knows how you are trying to reform your eating habits, it will make it that much more difficult to purchase certain food items. To cheat, you'll have to avoid her! Better yet, share with her some LOWFAT LIFESTYLE PRINCIPLES: her expanded knowledge of nutrition will make her a valuable asset to the store.

EXERCISE

EXERCISE

GUIDELINES FOR CHOOSING
YOUR EXERCISE PROGRAM

Your exercise prescription for physical activity is as important as a prescription for medication from your physician. You can assure a more successful exercise experience by considering the following steps:

1. THINK POSITIVELY. Too many people exercise as punishment for eating too much or drinking too much or to counter the effects of smoking, etc. Exercise is the best treat you can give your body and you should look at it as a positive experience.

2. KNOW YOURSELF. Are you a people person or a loner? What is your daily schedule and your best (or worst) time of the day? What kind of exercise have you enjoyed in the past? Look to your childhood. Activities that were enjoyable to you as a youth may satisfy you as an adult. Does competition spur or exhaust you? Do you work better with leadership or on your own?

3. PICK YOUR PRIME TIME. Consider your body's clock. Some people prefer to exercise at their low time of day. Some who dislike exercise choose their best time of day to undertake this activity. Interestingly, research has shown us that people who exercise late in the day tend to lose more body fat than those who exercise in the morning (despite similar regimens and caloric intake).

4. PICK THE EXERCISE STYLE OR SPORT RIGHT FOR YOU AND YOUR BODY. Unless you are a go-getter, you probably won't have a lot of success at basketball if you are five feet tall. Consider your body type and ability and choose your activity accordingly.

5. ESTABLISH REASONABLE GOALS. Goal setting in establishing your exercise and diet regimen is as important as goal setting in other areas of your life. Be sure you are realistic AND specific. Look at your present situation and past experiences.

Unrealistic expectations can get you into trouble. The 50% rule is often useful when setting goals. Cut your expectations in half and that may be truly realistic. For example, if you have never exercised before, a plan to walk three times a week for one hour is not realistic. Walking three times a week for fifteen to thirty minutes is realistic.

6. USE THE BEST EQUIPMENT. Choose well. Don't ever scrimp on the quality of your equipment. High quality equipment that fits your body type and size and that you enjoy using will serve as encouragement in your exercise program. If you are going to embark on a running program a good pair of shoes is a worthwhile investment. If you enjoy dressing for sport, do so, but remember it's not necessary to look like you stepped out of a magazine. It IS important to be comfortable.

7. LISTEN TO YOUR BODY. Your body is your own best signal as to whether you have chosen the best activity for you and your fitness level. You should remain invigorated two hours after your activity. If you are sore twenty-four hours after the activity it was too vigorous a workout for you. Recurring aches and pains from exercise are warning signals that you should not ignore.

While exercising, check your heart rate frequently to assure the correct pace. Remember the talk test. Avoid exercising at levels that make it impossible for you to carry on a conversation while you exercise.

8. GIVE YOURSELF TIME. Many people get discouraged and give up on their exercise program too easily. You can only get "hooked" by participating on a regular basis and it often takes several months before you SEE the results of your more active lifestyle. If you're having difficulty sticking with your regimen, re-evaluate yourself AND the activity.

9. OTHER CAVEATS:

INSERT VARIETY into your program. It cuts down on boredom, increases your options, decreases your chances for injury from overuse of a specific muscle group and makes you a more well-rounded person.

REMEMBER THE 10% RULE. Increase your workout by no more than 10% a week.

BUILD REST DAYS INTO YOUR PROGRAM. Rest days prevent a negative addiction to exercise (exercising beyond what is good for you). Once you are fit you can exercise three times a week and maintain your fitness level.

BUILD REWARDS INTO YOUR PROGRAM. Remember to reward yourself when you reach a goal. Ask others to pat you on the back for a job well done.

USE MOTIVATIONAL TOOLS. These are the little things that you can do to encourage yourself along the way.

RULES OF AEROBIC EXERCISE

A lowfat diet isn't enough. Aerobic exercise is essential in a total lifestyle program designed for optimum levels of fitness. Most of us know that aerobic exercise is important but a surprising number of people are not completely up to date on the subject.

Aerobic exercise can change the way your body works. It was first acclaimed for the cardiovascular changes it produced in the body...specifically a stronger heart, increased lung capacity, increased peripheral circulation and decreased blood pressure. Now we also know that aerobic exercise changes the way the body utilizes fat for energy, increases bone density, improves our sleep patterns, improves our mental well being, increases the body's mechanism to carry oxygen to muscles for work...the list goes on and on.

But what is an aerobic exercise? In order to be considered aerobic an exercise must conform to certain "rules". Since we like the easy way to remember things, consider the acronym FITT to help you remember the rules of aerobics.

F = FREQUENCY...you must exercise aerobically four days a week to increase your level of fitness.

I = INTENSITY...you must exercise at a pace sufficient to challenge your body. The best guide to whether you are exercising aerobically is to be working beyond normal limits and still be able to carry on a conversation. Extremely intense bursts of activity are NOT aerobic.

T = TIME...you must spend at least fifteen minutes at your activity without stopping, not even once.

T = TECHNIQUE...your aerobic activity must be a systemic exercise, one which uses the major muscle groups and affects your entire body favorably.

SOME POPULAR AEROBIC EXERCISES INCLUDE:

Aerobic Dance

Running

Bicycling

Cross country skiing

Jumping rope

Swimming

THESE EXERCISES ARE NOT AEROBIC:

Tennis

Handball

Racquetball

Calisthenics

Weight training

Golf

(P.S. This is only a partial list!)

REPETITIVE EXERCISES

Spot reducing is a fallacy!! The body does not pull fat from a specific area of the body just because you exercise it repeatedly. If you want to change the way your body looks you must undertake a regular program of aerobic exercise, which conditions the entire body, burns body fat and gives you an overall feeling of well-being, plus REPETITIVE EXERCISES, which are effective in strengthening individual muscle groups.

Repetitive exercise strengthens a muscle group by putting it on overload in much the same way weight-lifting builds strength when you lift a weight heavier than your muscle can easily support. Working a muscle in this way for a long period of time is what creates the "burn" exhorted by many fitness professionals. This uncomfortable feeling is a result of a buildup of lactic acid in the muscle and is the body's way of telling you to stop the movement. Repetitive exercise can tone and trim the body as the muscles strengthen, but remember that these muscles can't be seen if they are covered with too much body fat!

An open space with a foam-covered surface is the best place for repetitive exercise. The space allows freedom of movement and the foam helps protect the body from the injury that could be caused by excessive weight on a particular joint (particularly the back and the knees). A variety of exercises performed at a regular time every other day is the most effective regimen for strengthening individual muscle groups. We offer several on the following pages.

ARM AND SHOULDER EXERCISES

Standing with feet under shoulder line, knees slightly bent, swing arms like a pendulum front and back. Swing arms side to side in front of the body.

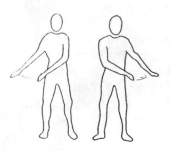 

Raise elbows to the shoulder line. Swing arms clockwise from the shoulder. Swing arms counter-clockwise from the shoulder. Swing arms in unison in a figure eight.

Emulate the motion of the swimmer's breast stroke and swimmer's crawl. With arms in front, forearms up, hands in fists, pull arms to back, push to front.

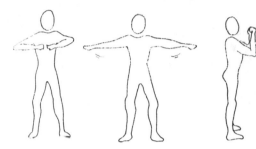

Standing straight, holding a towel with both hands in front of you at hip level, raise the towel over your head as you inhale deeply. Try to lower it behind your back as far down as you can go. (You may need to put your hands farther apart.) Return to the original position as you exhale.

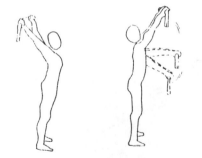

Place your fingertips on your shoulders, elbows to the sides, and slowly rotate your elbows in large circles. Reverse the direction.

THIGH EXERCISES

Standing with feet under the shoulder line, toes turned out, knees bent slightly, lift the left heel off the ground 16 times. Repeat with other heel. To progress, lift the entire foot off the floor.

Lie on the floor with knees bent and the soles of the feet touching. The feet can be on the floor or in the air. Keep the feet together and bring the knees together and apart a total of 16 times.

Lie on the floor with the legs extended straight up. Try to keep the knees in a locked position. Point the toes and alternate the feet quickly with right in front, then left in front. "Beat" the feet in this position 16 times. Flex the ankles and extend the heels to the ceiling. Turn the toes out, then in, a total of 16 times. Be sure the rotation occurs from the hips.

Lie on the floor with the left leg bent, foot close to the buttocks. Extend the right leg to a straight position with the toe turned out, then in, for a total of 16 times. Be sure to keep the back connected to the floor. Repeat with the left leg.

Sit on the floor with the working leg extended in front of you, the knee locked and the toe pointed and turned toward the outside of the body. Bend the other leg underneath. Lift, then lower the extended leg about 8 inches off the floor (you may need to support your body by resting on your hands behind you). Repeat a minimum of 8 times, maximum of 16 times. Repeat with other leg.

As you get stronger, release some of the weight on the hands, remembering to support yourself with the abdominals!

Lie on your left side. Bend your left knee. Keep the right leg over the left foot. The knee should be straight and facing forward. Raise and lower the straight leg a minimum of 8 times. As your strength progresses, lift your upper body so your head is resting on your arm, then support your weight by your bent elbow, then by your left hand. Repeat to the other side.

Using the wall or a chair for balance, stand on your right foot. With the left leg straight, toe pointed inward, bring the left leg across your right leg and hold for 8 seconds. Repeat to the other side. Alternate for a total of 5 times.

Lie on your left side with both knees bent, body supported on the elbow. Lift then lower the right leg a minimum of 8 times. As your strength progresses, raise the upper body so it is supported by the left hand. Repeat to the other side.

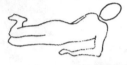 

Lie on your left side with both knees bent, body supported on the elbow. Lift the right knee about 6 inches, then extend the right foot forward about 5 inches, then back to the bent position. Repeat 8 times. As your strength progresses, raise the upper body so it is supported by the left hand. Repeat to the other side.

Lie on your left side with both knees bent, body supported on the elbow. Bring the right leg to the chest. Grab the right foot with the right hand and slowly pull the foot behind you to stretch the front of the right thigh.

To stretch further, gently push the right hip forward, then release, a total of 8 times. DO NOT DO THIS EXERCISE IF IT HURTS YOUR KNEE!! Repeat to the other side.

Lie on your left side with both knees bent. Bring your right knee to your chest, grab the right toe and push the heel forward to straighten the right leg. If you cannot straighten your leg in this position extend it upward to the ceiling or grab the ankle for support. You should feel the stretch behind the leg, in the calf muscle. Repeat to the other side.

Lying on the left side with weight supported on the hip and elbow, cross the right foot over the body with the foot resting as close to the left hip as possible. Lift and lower the extended left leg a minimum of 8 times. Be sure the left leg extends straight out from the hip, not forward or backward. Repeat to the other side.

In a seated position, with the left leg bent in front of you, cross the right leg over the left with the foot close to the hip. Hold the right leg and pull the knee toward the opposite shoulder, pushing right hip into floor. Repeat.

BUTTOCKS EXERCISES

It's important when doing "buttocks" exercises to think about isolating the muscles that you are working. Try to be conscious of leg, hip, and buttocks work and avoid extending the motion to become "back" work.

On all fours, with head to chest, bring the knee to the chest then extend the leg straight back with a pointed toe. Repeat a minimum of 8 times. Continue the motion with the ankle flexed. Repeat to the other side.

On all fours, with head to chest, extend the right leg straight back. Moving the rest of the body as little as possible, lift the leg straight up, then down, while pushing the buttock against the leg to prevent a hyperextension of the lower back.

The previous two exercises may be combined into one exercise often described as the "donkey kick". This exercise is dangerous if done in a swinging motion. Remember, "knee to chest, extend the leg, lift the leg against the buttock, lower the leg", then repeat.

With weight resting on knees and elbows (a modified all fours position), extend the leg up and behind with the knee and ankle flexed at a 90 degree angle. While keeping the head to the chest push the heel to the ceiling. Think about the motion of hitting a nail into the ceiling. Repeat 16 times. Repeat with other leg.

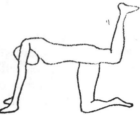

While lying on the back with the feet on the floor push the weight into the heels to lift the buttocks toward the ceiling. Repeat this movement a minimum of 8, maximum of 16 times. A more progressive exercise is to lift the buttocks to the ceiling then bring the legs together and apart, together and apart, a minimum of 8 times.

ABDOMINALS

The abdominal exercises we've provided here strengthen the abdominals which provide very important support in maintaining proper posture and "protecting the back" from injury. As you progress through these movements remember to focus on the abdominal muscles. Any time you do an exercise where you are lying on your back it's imperative you precede the movement with the thought "USE THE ABDOMINALS TO PRESS THE LOWER BACK INTO THE FLOOR FIRST." Remember also to breathe regularly through every movement.

Sit on the floor with knees bent, hands on knees. Keeping your chin tucked to your chest, begin to exhale and slowly lower your back, then your shoulders toward the floor. When your stomach muscles start to "pooch", you've gone too far! Return to the sitting position and repeat up to 8 times.

Lie on your back with knees bent and feet flat on the floor. Inhale. As you exhale, press the small of your back to the floor and lift your head and shoulders off the floor. Do not come up any farther than a position where your stomach muscles start to "pooch". Repeat up to 8 times.

Lying on the floor with the right knee bent and the left leg extended straight up in the air (preferably with the knee in a locked position), press your lower back into the floor. As you exhale reach with your right hand to your left ankle, then lie back. Repeat a minimum of 8 times. Change legs and repeat.

Lying on the floor with both legs extended to the ceiling, press the lower back into the floor and reach toward the feet with the arms extended, pulling the whole upper torso off the floor.

Lying on the floor with the arms by the side and the palms of the hands resting on the floor, push your weight into your hands to lift your hips off the floor. Be sure to flatten your abdominals to give yourself some extra strength. Remember to exhale as you push and inhale as you lower.

Lying on the back with the hands tucked under the hips to give them a slight elevation, put both feet straight up in the air. While keeping your lower back pressed to the floor alternately lower first the right then the left leg. When you begin to feel tired in your back or abdominals it's time for a break!

Lying on the back with the legs straight up, arms overhead, scissors the legs out to the side then bring them back together, crossing one another center so they cross in front... first right in front, then left in front. After you have repeated this movement several times, add another. As the legs move apart swing the arms forward and through the open legs. Think "press the abdomen into the floor" each time you lift. Remember, exhale as you lift, inhale as you lower.

Lying on the back with the weight on the elbows, bring both knees to the chest. Flex the ankles and alternately kick the left then the right foot forward. Repeat a minimum of 16 times.

BACK

Sitting with the soles of the feet together and extended as far out in front of the body as possible without the soles of the feet coming apart, drop your chin to your chest. You may feel a tingling sensation as your upper back and neck muscles stretch out.

If you like, you can add the weight of your arms to this exercise by putting the hands on the crown of the head and letting the elbows drop forward. Take 4 deep breaths in this position. With each exhalation try to round the back a little more.

Put your hands underneath your heels to elevate them slightly and to provide leverage as you pull your body forward toward the feet. You can lead with your chin with this one. Think "chin over feet". Take 4 deep breaths in this position. As you breathe out try to bring your chin closer to the feet. This helps stretch out the lower back.

Sitting cross-legged, relax your upper body and try to round over your feet. Take 4 deep breaths in this position. Repeat the exercise with the other leg crossed on top!

RELAXATION

Finish any exercise session with the kinds of gentle stretches your body needs most.

The final movement for an exercise session should include some relaxation techniques. Lie on the floor with the arms by the side, palms up. Pull your knees toward your body so the soles of your feet are flat on the floor. Let the knees fall together so they are resting against one another. This is called a neutral position because each part of the body is resting against another part or against the floor.

Do some deep breathing exercises in this position or listen to some quiet music or try to mentally transport yourself to a place you feel quiet. Give yourself some quiet time...YOU DESERVE IT.

TO STRETCH OR NOT TO STRETCH
THAT IS THE QUESTION

There continues to be a lot of controversy surrounding the subject of stretching. To stretch or not to stretch... that is the question. I have to tell you that I do not have the answer. I do stretch everyday and my more flexible than normal body shows it. I need that flexibility to perform optimally as the physical leader of an aerobic dance workout. High kicks, side reaches, ceiling stretches are a part of MY everyday life. I also run every day but I do not stretch before running; instead, I warm up for running by starting with a brisk walk, then a slow jog, then a faster jog.

Much of the back pain experienced by the population of this country is described as inorganic (meaning there is no demonstrable lesion or injury). Pain anywhere in the body is an indication that injury has occurred whether it is visible or not. People who have back problems are almost universally encouraged to embark on a program which improves abdominal and back strength and increases overall body flexibility. Resistance to a stretching regimen by people who are physically active makes little sense and resistance by inactive people makes no sense at all.

The issue may NOT be to stretch or not to stretch but rather how LITTLE we need to stretch in order to make a difference in the way our bodies respond to movements that are out of the realm of our everyday movement patterns.

A muscle is very much like a rubber band. Stretch it too far and it snaps back into place. That is why bouncy (ballistic) stretches are discouraged in any sport regimen. On the other hand, a slow (static) stretch performed when a muscle is warm can be relaxing to the body and make the muscle fibers aware of a different kind of tension that can enhance our every move.

When a muscle goes through a repetitive movement (such as running) it gets very strong. Sometimes it also gets very tight. It may over-contract following the run, in response to the work load that has been put on it during the workout. Stretching out the leg muscles can reawaken muscle fibers to decrease tension.

In the same way fitness personnel encourage us to live a well rounded fitness existence, not focusing on one discipline but participating in a variety of activities, our approach to stretching should not be limited to only one muscle group. A gentle program of stretching of all the major muscle groups can make you feel better.

We may need to take a lesson from our animal friends. If you watch animals you will quickly become aware of how often they stretch. If you become aware of your own body, you will realize that unconsciously you stretch often throughout the day to relieve tension, get a second start on a project or, accompanied by a deep breath, simply wake up and get moving again.

The key to stretching is to taking it easy. There seems to be some inside demand telling our bodies we must go the limit. Stretching should never hurt. It should feel wonderful. You never want to stretch beyond your most comfortable limits. Over-stretching can be just as detrimental as no stretching at all.

Remember that rubber band. Don't overextend those muscles. Treat your body gently if you want it to perform to optimum capacity for the rest of your life. A regular aerobic exercise program combined with a minimum of strength work and a gentle stretching program takes very little time during your day and will make you feel wonderful.

A FINAL WORD

TAKE CARE OF THIS WONDERFUL MACHINE
WE SO TAKE FOR GRANTED AND IT WILL
SERVE YOU WELL YOUR WHOLE LIFE!

BOOKS! BOOKS! AND MORE BOOKS!

Do you find you want to devour all you can about each new experience you undertake? When I added jogging to my fitness regimen I suddenly had an interest in reading about running shoes. After getting a new bicycle, finding a book to learn how to care for it was a high priority.

Through the years I've read all of the diet books and most of the exercise books that have hit the market. These years of reading have helped to develop a critical eye for determining the readability and value of books that will enhance your ability to adopt a lowfat lifestyle. The following list is by no means complete and does not include some very fine books that go into greater scientific detail on the subjects of nutrition and exercise. There are hundreds of books on the shelf related to fitness but no one book that tells it all.

Most of the books listed here are available at any bookstore. If they must be special ordered from a supplier, the most recent price and a mailing address is supplied.

Remember, books — even this one — are excellent tools for motivation only if they can be used on a regular basis (most of my diet books have ended up on the shelf or in the rummage box because I finally have learned that diets don't work). Hopefully, this list will get you started!

R.G.

245

EXERCISE AND FITNESS

AEROBICS, THE AEROBICS WAY, AEROBICS FOR WOMEN, THE NEW AEROBICS and THE AEROBICS PROGRAM FOR TOTAL WELL BEING by Ken Cooper. Ken Cooper started this whole aerobic exercise movement and though his books emphasize the use of his point plan they have good information in them. In my opinion the last book is the best.

FIT OR FAT? by Covert Bailey. Without a doubt this is the bible for anyone who needs encouragement to embark on an aerobic exercise program. It explains how aerobic exercise can change your metabolism and brings a very complex subject to readers in understandable terms. The paperback version has been on and off the best seller list for the last few years. It is inexpensive and entertaining and is second only to hearing Covert Bailey speak in person.

HOW TO KEEP SLENDER AND FIT AFTER THIRTY by Bonnie Prudden. This book has been around for a long time and is still an excellent reference. It emphasizes muscular fitness and flexibility.

HOW TO LOWER YOUR FAT THERMOSTAT by Remington, Fisher and Parent. This book is not an "easy read" but is not too technical either. It covers lots of information on diet and exercise and emphasizes the set point theory for maintaining realistic weight goals.

NUTRITION, WEIGHT CONTROL AND EXERCISE by F. I. Katch and W. D. McArdle. This thick paperback is a textbook at many colleges and universities. It is very readable and provides a well-rounded presentation of all the facets of these subjects. It is for the reader who wants more depth on the subject without getting lost in a lot of technical mumble jumble!

THE AMERICAN HEART ASSOCIATION HEARTBOOK. You can really learn a lot about your body with this book. It emphasizes the cardiac side of life, including hazards of smoking, diet and nutrition, exercise, how the heart functions and heart disease. It's recommended reading for anyone who wants to understand more about cardiovascular fitness.

THE COMPLETE BOOK OF RUNNING, THE SECOND BOOK OF RUNNING by James Fixx. Both of these are best sellers and cover almost everything you would want or need to know about running.

THE SPORTS DOCTOR'S FITNESS BOOK FOR WOMEN by John Marshall. Available in hardback only, this is an excellent book for both the recreational and serious athlete by an experienced sports medicine physician. It is very complete and will enable you to assess your fitness level.

THE Y'S WAY TO A HEALTHY BACK by Alexander Melleby. The Y has a very successful back program that was developed by an authority on back care. Hans Kraus, M.D. This book puts the program on paper and is useful for those who have minor back problems.

NUTRITION AND WEIGHT CONTROL

DIETS DON'T WORK by Bob Schwarts. This workbook approach to the "problem" of dieting is printed by Breakthru Publishing and deals with self awareness and the behavior modification aspects of dietary changes to assure permanent weight loss.

DIET FOR A SMALL PLANET by F. M. Lappe. Be sure to buy the revised edition of this highly respected book as Ms. Lappe has altered her original views on the necessity of combining proteins for a balanced diet. Highly recommended.

DIETARY GOALS FOR THE UNITED STATES. Available from the Superintendent of Documents, U.S. Government Printing Office, Washington, D.C. 20402. Stock No. 052-070-04376-8. It costs $2.30 to obtain the complete report of the Senate Select Committee on Nutrition and Human Needs. It's a typical government publication but is interesting reading.

EVERYTHING YOU ALWAYS WANTED TO KNOW ABOUT NUTRITION by David Reuben, M.D. Dr. Reuben's best-selling book uses a question and answer format and "plain talk" to discuss vitamins, minerals, trace elements, fats, carbohydrates, proteins and sugar.

THE FIT-OR-FAT TARGET DIET by Covert Bailey, M.S. Covert Bailey does it again. This book utilizes a target theory developed by Bailey as a nutritional education program that emphasizes a balanced diet low in fat, low in sugar and high in fiber. Using this system can give you an understanding of foods that can assure permanent weight control, loss of body fat and implementation of U.S. Dietary Goals. Although it is easy to understand, it will require more concentration than FIT OR FAT. We recommend one of Bailey's Target Diet workshops to give you a quick start on this exciting new way of looking at foods.

FOOD VALUES OF PORTIONS COMMONLY USED by Jean A.T. Pennington and Helen Nichols Church. This is a classic and provides a quick and accurate reference book for commonly eaten foods.

JANE BRODY'S NUTRITION BOOK by Jane Brody. Called "a lifetime guide to good eating for better health and weight control", this large but easy to read volume touches all areas of nutrition.

NUTRITIVE VALUE OF FOODS, a publication of the U.S. Department of Agriculture, Home and Garden Bulletin Number 72. This is a table of nutritive values for commonly used foods. It is available in most college bookstores or from The Superintendent of Documents, U.S. Government Printing Office, Washington, D.C. 20402.

RATING THE DIETS by Consumer Guide. As usual, they tell it like it is. Unfortunately, they do not always have an evaluation of the latest fad diet...you have to wait for next year's edition!

THE DIETER'S COMPLETE GUIDE TO CALORIES, CARBOHYDRATES, SODIUM, FATS AND CHOLES-TEROL by the editors of Consumer Guide. This handbook should be in everyone's kitchen. Look up a food BEFORE you eat it to find out about its nutritive value.

THE PRITIKIN PERMANENT WEIGHT-LOSS MANUAL by Nathan Pritikin. This book is an update of The Pritikin Program for Diet and Exercise and includes many lowfat recipes. The Pritikin Centers teach overweight and high risk cardiac patients how to change their eating habits to save their lives. The book is interesting. The diet is TOO low in fat for the average consumer.

COOKBOOKS

Be sure when you seek out lowfat cookbooks that they are not merely low in cholesterol. Cholesterol is just one kind of fat and we've been shocked at how high in fat some so-called "lowfat cookbooks" are! We've checked these out and think they're good.

BEAUTIFUL FOOD FOR YOUR BEAUTIFUL BODY by Jeanette Silveira Burke. A very thick (250 pages) paperback that includes commentary by the author who has a B.A. and M.S. degree in home economics. Available by mail for $9.95 plus $1.05 postage and handling. Write to J. Burke, 5804 E. Hamilton, Fresno, California, 93727.

DON'T TELL 'EM IT'S GOOD FOR 'EM by Nancy Baggett, Ruth Glick and Gloria Kaufer Greene. The authors of this cookbook of 250 recipes and tips know you can't change your family's eating habits overnight. They use an interesting system called Nutri-Steps to gradually modify recipes to become lower in fat and sugar.

LAUREL'S KITCHEN by Laurel Robertson, Carol Flinders and Bronwen Godfrey. This is a vegetarian cookbook but not necessarily low in fat so be sure to check out the recipes. It is an excellent source for meatless meals.

LEAN LIFE CUISINE by Eve Lowry and Carla Mulligan. This small cookbook has only 30 very creative recipes but each is analyzed for its fiber, fat, protein and carbohydrate content and contains a vitamin/mineral graph of its ingredients. We especially liked the lowfat avocado salad dressing. Send $4.50 to Carla Mulligan, P. O. Box 16323, S. Lake Tahoe, California 95706.

NO SALT NO SUGAR NO FAT COOKBOOK by Nitty Gritty Cookbooks. This small cookbook (120 recipes) is available in many health food and specialty stores for $5.95. The back cover says satisfaction is guaranteed! Nitty Gritty Productions, P. O. Box 5457-N, Concord, California, 94524.

TARGET DIET RECIPES FOR FIT OR FAT FOLKS by Lee Bishop and Covert Bailey. This book is a compendium of the many recipes that were sent to the Bailey Clinic and then tested and reviewed in Bailey and Bishop kitchens. It also contains supplementary information on how to establish realistic weight goals and lots of kitchen hints for cooking the lowfat way! $4.50 plus $1.50 postage and handling from B & B Enterprises, P. O. Box 16590, S. Lake Tahoe, CAlifornia, 95706. Quantity discounts are available.

THE I LOVE TO EAT BUT HATE TO DIET COOKBOOK by Joan Mary Alimonti. 275 recipes that are practical. Write to Asta Productions, P. O. Box 3238, Walnut Creek, California, 94598.

DEFINITIONS

AEROBIC
This describes an organism that needs oxygen (or air) for energy or life.

AEROBIC EXERCISE
Those exercises or sports activities that stimulate heart and lung activity for a sufficient period of time to produce beneficial changes in the body, e.g. running, cycling, jogging, crewing, cross-country skiing, swimming, aerobic dancing.

ANAEROBIC
This describes an organism that can live without the presence of oxygen.

CALORIE
A measure of a unit of heat or energy.

CHOLESTEROL
A fat-like substance found in all animal fats, bile, skin and brain tissue.

DEFICIENCY
The lack of a specific nutrient or nutrients.

DIET
A selection of food. Unfortunately the word has come to mean a food selection to which a person is restricted in a weight loss program.

FAT SOLUBLE VITAMIN
A vitamin able to dissolve in fats or or oils.

FATTY ACIDS Substances that give fats their different flavors, textures and melting points. They may be saturated (of animal origin) or unsaturated (of vegetable origin).

FIBER That part of food that is not digested by the body, such as the skin of an apple.

FITNESS The American Heart Association defines fitness as "the ability to carry out daily activities without undue fatigue and to respond to physical and emotional stress without negative effects on the human body".

GLUCOSE The simplest form of sugar which is assimilated in the body; blood sugar.

GLYCOGEN The form in which carbohydrates are stored in the body.

GRAINS The seeds of various grasses such as wheat, rice, rye, oats and barley.

LEAN BODY MASS The weight of muscles, bones, hair, organs and tissue — in other words, everything except fat and air.

LEGUMES Plants that have edible seeds within a pod. These include peas, beans, lentils and peanuts.

MAXIMUM WORKING HEART RATE	The absolute maximum pace you should allow yourself to work in an aerobic workout. To work at higher levels serves no useful purpose and could be dangerous.
MINIMUM WORKING HEART RATE	The minimum number of beats in 1 minute which will elicit the beneficial changes incurred through aerobic work. You should work to this level or higher. (Note: For some people even a small elevation over their resting heart rate may be sufficient to be described as aerobic.)
NUTRIENT	A substance needed by a living thing to maintain life, health and reproduction.
OBESITY	Having excessive amounts of body fat for your frame.
OVERFAT	A man who carries more than 15% of his weight as fat or a woman who carries more than 22% of her weight as fat.
OVERWEIGHT	A term used to describe a person who weighs more than recommended on standard height-weight charts.
PULSE OR HEART RATE	The number of times your heart beats in 1 minute.

RECOMMENDED DAILY ALLOWANCE	The amount of nutrients suggested by the National Research Council as being necessary to maintain life processes in most healthy persons.
RESTING HEART RATE	The number of times your heart beats in 1 minute before you get up in the morning or after you have been sitting quietly for at least 20 minutes.
SOMATOTYPING	A way of describing body types. ECTOMORPH — a lean and angular body type; MESOMORPH — a muscular body type; ENDOMORPH — a more rounded, soft body.
STRESS	Anytime your body or mind is subjected to an experience "out of the ordinary" it can be described as stress. Stress can therefore be a very exhilarating experience and many people perform well when under mental or physical pressure. Problems occur when there is an overload of your circuits to produce what we know as distress. When this occurs you may become more irritable and experience periods of poor judgement. The stress interferes with efficient management of your life!!
TARGET ZONE	The range that measures between 60% and 80% of your maximum working heart rate. Exercising in this zone guarantees the gain of aerobic benefits without overstressing the body.

INDEX

258   *Index*